The Externsteine:

Europe's greatest Celtic site

Damien   Pryor

Understanding its cultural & historical significance for the Celts, the Caesars, the Teutonic tribes & Charlemagne's Empire

Also available by this author:
The Great Pyramid and the Sphinx
Stonehenge: The essential guide to its purpose and context
Lalibela in thirteenth century Ethiopia
The tropical zodiac, its origin and validity

The author asserts the moral right to be regarded as the author of
this book

CONTENTS

THE EXTERNSTEINE

Chapter One: Background & History

Introduction

Deep inside the dense forests that cover the hills and wide plains
of northern Germany, a remarkable cluster of sandstone rocks
towers upwards into the sky, far above the oak and fir trees.
Here four thousand years ago, the ancient Celtic-Germanic
people once lived and worshipped their mysterious gods. Then
as the Celts faded from the pages of history, about the time that
Greece civilisation reached its Golden Age, this area became
home to the Teutonic tribes. They continued many of the
religious practises and beliefs of the Celts whilst they fought
against the militant imperialism of the Roman Caesars. Finally,
in the eighth century, Charlemagne began to extend his Christian
empire over the lands of the Teutonic people. Gradually the
Holy Roman Empire spread across the forests of northern
Germany absorbing the Germanic tribes, and around 1100 AD,
with the Christian church-state dominating Europe, the Bishop
of Paderborn encouraged monks and priests to use the
Externsteine rocks for ecclesiastical purposes.

An inscription on the wall of one of the chambers informs us
that in 1115 AD the bishop of Paderborn, Heinrich von Werl,
consecrated a chamber here to Christ. It is rumoured that he also
ordered the construction of some of the chambers here, as well.
Historical documents do confirm that the Bishop built a church
at Krukenberg (near Helmarshausen) that was designed to
replicate a church at Golgotha in Jerusalem. But did the Church
create the features of this site; is this just a medieval church site?
Johannes Mundhenk, in his detailed and careful study of
references to the Externsteine in the Middle Ages, has found that
it was mentioned by a Lutheran priest, Hermann Hamelmann,
who reports that "the Externsteine is a very old monument, to
which writers from earlier times referred, and where
Charlemagne dedicated a pagan idol to God." (1) But this
clergyman does not say just to which earlier writers he is
referring.

Recently a number of scientists carried out extensive research here, to establish the date of the burn marks found in some chambers. Their research overturned the conservative view that this extraordinary site was principally the work of the medieval church. For some of the earlier fires that caused these burn marks were dated to about 700 AD and a little later. So the chambers were not created by the 12th century church; this theory is wrong.

Already around 700 AD, it was the earlier inhabitants, the non-Christian Teutonic people who were using this site at this time. But a few burn marks on the walls of some chambers, are only a minor feature. They tell us almost nothing about the motivation that brought the Teutonic people to this site. To find out just how old this site really is, and what its fascinating features mean, we have to really take note of what we find here.

Wandering amongst these tall rock outcrops, the visitor is startled by the appearance of the faces of people, or the shapes of mythic animals like dragons, apparently formed quite accidentally, by the fissures and cracks and bulges of the huge rocks. And a visitor is intrigued to see, set into the wall of one of the chambers an opening, near ground level, which scientists have discovered is aligned to the midsummer sunrise. And looking up at another rocky tower, some 20 metres above the ground an opening can be seen in the wall of a strange chamber; a chamber that was once fully enclosed, and very difficult to access.

This opening is in fact also aligned to the midsummer sunrise, for on that morning the sun's rays shine in for a little while and illumine a strange ugly face on the rear wall. We start to suspect that these features take us far back into history, many, many centuries before the Hellenistic Age began. Was the medieval church only the last of several groups of people to use this site?

2

1 MAP of Area

The Externsteine site and Kalkriese, the site of the Varus battle

In this remote forest area, the Celts established their greatest sacred site, ca. 3,000 BC.

In the Hellenistic Age, it became the Teutonic tribes' most sacred site. It was influential in Rome's worst ever defeat, in the Varus battle in 9 AD.

In 772 AD it was attacked by Charlemagne soldiers, causing the 33 yr Wittekind uprising.

In the Middle Ages it was acquired by the church.

In the 20th century it became a nationa park

Pict. adapted from: www.freeworldmaps/europa

3

Further research has discovered that a conical rod put into the hole of this chamber points precisely to the position of the lunar node, a cycle covering 18.6 years, when the moon reaches its greatest influence. And a set of stone steps in front of another tower gives direct observation of the sunrise on the autumn and spring equinox. Now these astronomical observation points are an identifying feature of the Celtic people, they are similar to the Megalithic people of England who constructed Stonehenge. But only very recently has it been realized that the ancient inhabitants of Europe were both capable of sophisticated astronomical observation and felt deeply impelled to construct sites that facilitated this.

It was a recent discovery at another German site, a few hundred kilometres away, at Nebra near Goseck, that demonstrated that all over central and northern Europe, the Celtic priesthoods were really focused on precise observation of solar and lunar rhythms. An ancient bronze disc was found, with some gold-leaf embossing, which dates from about 1,500 BC. It showed the Pleiades, as they appeared 3,600 years ago, and it also showed how to harmonize the discrepancy between the 12 solar months and the 13 lunar months.

Long ages ago, people with a deep religious interest in celestial influences such as solar and lunar cycles, created the type of features seen at the Externsteine. Many other features are here, telling us that in north Germany at the Externsteine, in bygone ages, the ancient Celts once established a prominent sacred site. But later on, as the Celts disappeared from the pages of history and the Teutonic tribes people lived in these forests, they added other features to the site. For example, excavations in the 1930's revealed that there was charcoal material in the deeper layers of the soil. This is a strong indication that once a large wooden object was standing up in front of one of the columns. This was almost certainly a version of the supreme symbol of the northern Germanic-Celtic peoples. This was a tall wooden column with some simple carvings on it. This was called the Irmin Column, and it represented Creation, which to these ancient people was a multi-

4

layered cosmos. This column was probably destroyed by an attack on the site in very early medieval times.

Another fascinating feature of the Externsteine is a sarcophagus carved out of a large rock, and set in its own stone chamber, with an arched ceiling. The usual interpretation of this is again a medieval feature, a symbolic Christian grave, designed to piously replicate the grave of Jesus. But as we have already noted, the site in general is not of medieval origin. But was perhaps only this feature created by the church? We shall explore this question in detail later, but for now we note that a recent discovery in southern Bulgaria (or Thrace) in the Eastern Rhodopes, has shed new light on this sarcophagus, affirming that it derives from the ancient Celtic-Germanic peoples.

The Celtic world is of great interest to many people today, because the Celts had a deep feeling for nature spirituality. This included influences from the stars, the sun, and the moon, especially at solstice and equinox times, as the Nebra disc and many megalithic sites in Germany and Britain show. But the ancient Celts of western and northern Europe, living long before the Hellenistic Age, left little behind to explain their fascination in these things, but some knowledge has been learnt about this from later Celtic cultures.

As we explore the features of this site carefully, noting what academic studies and scientific research projects have found, we shall find that the Externsteine was probably the most revered Celtic site in Europe. When clearly understood, its features offer a treasure trove of insights into the spiritual beliefs of the ancient Celts, and also the later Teutonic tribes. And yet, this site is hardly known outside Germany, and in Germany itself much confusion prevails about its many fascinating features. It has been extensively ignored for political-cultural reasons; or has been the subject of ungrounded emotional attitudes.

A more significant influence in keeping the Externsteine so little appreciated, is that in mainstream archaeology the possibility of any ancient site having sophisticated alignments to solar or lunar cycles is still resisted, despite the careful research of mainstream astronomers confirming that this is often the situation. The Nebra disc discovery has alerted archaeologists to the need to widen their perspective here. A striking example of the need to do this was the embarrassment amongst archaeologists in Britain in regard to Stonehenge, back in the 1960's, when an American astronomer asserted that amongst its features are astronomical alignments. They objected angrily in print, but some months later, they had to acknowledge that the astronomers were in fact correct. For the foremost of British astronomers, Sir Fred Hoyle, confirmed these astronomical alignments. The discovery of the Nebra disc with its precise astronomical focus has likewise widened everyone's eyes to the intense interest of pre-literate peoples in celestial influences and rhythms.

The various features of the Externsteine are derived from an ancient holistic attitude. But to our modern humanistic attitude this is not easily perceived, so the full significance of this site has not been widely understood. This confusion has opened the door to many often ungrounded speculations about the site. Hence there is little awareness today of its actual cultural significance in terms of understanding Celtic spirituality and also the early Celtic-Germanic (Teutonic) religious life. The Externsteine did have a significant role in early German history. The Externsteine did play a major role in the development of central and northern European spirituality. The beautiful mythic texts of the Edda are a later expression of this ancient spiritual worldview.

As we shall see, the Externsteine started as an ancient and primitive Celtic site, approximately three millennia before the Hellenistic Age, but was later assimilated by the old Teutonic tribes people, some centuries before the Christian era. In this second phase of its history, it played a central role in the pre-history of the later German nation. The tribal priestess and her assistants at the Externsteine were very likely responsible for the most decisive military defeat the Roman Empire ever suffered, at the famous battle of Varus. That is, the priests of the Teutonic peoples would have strengthened the determination of the tribe

6

to defend themselves from the Romans. The Teutonic people had assimilated the Externsteine into their own religious practises as the Celtics faded out. It no doubt became the greatest of the Teutonic religious sites. The defeat of the Roman army 2,000 years ago played a major role in preventing central and northern Europe from becoming Roman colonies – thus ensuring the development of an independent European culture, north of the Alps, entirely separate from Italy.

The Externsteine is also the place where in the 9th century, 800 years after the wars with the Roman Caesars, Charlemagne, the Holy Roman Emperor, carried out his militant campaign to subdue the Saxons. As we shall see, he attacked this ancient sacred site with its astronomical observatory, its ritual chambers, and its wonderful works of art. This was done in an attempt to destroy the will of the Saxons to resist his wish to bring them into Christianity. So, part of the research into the Externsteine involves considering whether the historical records of the Frankish Empire were sanitized to delete reference to this action.

And in terms of its place in the history of Art, the Externsteine with its large and striking Christian relief rock carving occupies a significant place. It is the most significant Christian artwork of its kind ever made in Europe. This carving is also the most strikingly ignored of all great and prominent Christian artworks, and incorrectly dated to the 12th century, based on assumptions about the involvement of Bishop Heinrich of Paderborn here. Sociologically, the importance of this carving is huge. In terms of a study of European history, and of the sociology of religion, it is the single most significant example of Christian art forcefully placed inside a 'pagan' sacred site, to persuade a conquered (and outraged) people to peacefully accept the Christianization of their culture.

And yet, most people outside Germany whom you ask about the Externsteine will say that they have never heard of it, or have only a vague idea about it. Whether they are students or teachers of Celtic civilisation, of ancient sacred sites, of Christian Art, of

Religious History, of the Sociology of Religion, of Charlemagne and the Frankish Empire, of early German history, or indeed of the Roman Empire and its wars in 'Germania'. Yet the Externsteine has substantial significance for all of the above fields of knowledge. So let's find out about this amazing site.

Location, and description

Geologically the Externsteine consists of five large, very tall rock towers amongst a distinctive outcrop in the beautiful Teutoburger Forest (in German, the Teutoburger Wald). Geologists report that this outcrop is actually several hundred metres long, although most of them don't rise up above ground level. In 1926 this area, encompassing 140 hectares, was made into a protected national park, and has about 10 km of walking tracks. This site is located in north-western Germany, the two nearest towns of any size being Detmold and Paderborn. The village of Horn-Bad Meinberg is quite close and accommodation is available there, and there is a restaurant on the site itself, see the map of the general area. A new Tourist Center is being built there to facilitate one's appreciation of the site.

The German name for this site, 'Externsteine' is of unknown origin, the common assumption today being that it probably comes from the name of a nearby mountainous area, the "Egge", and means 'the stone of Egge'. However, the first documented reference to the site in old German texts, from 1093 AD, calls it the 'Agisterstein'; and this may possibly mean the 'stone with the dragon cave'. This would indicate the feeling in the local populace in medieval times that the site has something 'uncanny' about it. A good guide on the Internet to exploring the general area, but only in German is available from the "Eggegebirgsverein."[1]

Five of the tall sandstone outcrops form columns tower up as high as 120 ft (40 m), and there are also a few other large rocks in the general vicinity which are of interest too, see illustration 1. The site is a popular tourist attraction, with busloads of people

---

[1] German text only: www.eggegebirgsverein.de/service/wanderwege im Eggeraum

visiting every day; between a half million and one million tourists come here each year (at the summer and winter solstice the place is really buzzing with people, already before dawn). The rock columns have a fantastical, striking appearance, see Illustration One.

This striking appearance of the columns is normally understood to be the result of weathering, however there are very substantial signs that the strange appearance and ambience of the rocks is also partly the result of them having been shaped in places, by human hands, long ages ago. Now here we already (!) enter into a disputed aspect of this site, and the Externsteine is controversial for many reasons. Are these features made by humans or by Nature? Anyway, it is fascinating to experience them.

And the Externsteine is a fascinating place, at the solstice or equinox or on May Day, large crowds of people descend on the site. Once you go there, you will feel how electrical and atmospheric it is. The rock columns have a number of staircases hewn from the stone, some leading nowhere (the site was partially destroyed 1,200 years ago). But a suspension bridge now leads up to a mysterious chamber, and inside the main column (rock 1) there are several grottos.

On the outside of this very wide column is an extraordinary carved scene, or, rather, scenes. Here we plunge again into the controversy, for the Christian scene here, of the Deposition of Christ from the Cross, unique in all of Europe, also has below it another scene that is very likely an ancient Celtic scene, not a Christian artwork.

A careful observation of various rocks around the site reveals what appear to be the outlines of mythical beings associated with the nature spirituality of the Celts. In addition, the evidence is very clear that the Externsteine also served the Druids as a kind of 'astronomical observatory'.

2 **A photograph of the Externsteine**, showing its great rock towers and general layout. The wobble stone on top of one tower, and the bridge across to the special chamber on the tallest tower. To the right are the two carved reliefs; the sarcophagus is not visible .

10

It is this aspect that gives a clue to the real origin and age of this site, as we shall see. To be able to benefit the most from a visit to this site, or to understand its role in the cultural life of earlier times, it is obviously important to know its significance. So, we need to know what evidence there is of any really ancient usage, in other words, we need to know when, and therefore why, this rock outcrop was made into a sacred site.

Well, that means knowing what its purpose was, and that means finding out when it was set up as a sacred site, and by whom it was established. That's where the controversy starts – at the beginning! With only a few historical records about the site surviving from ancient times, it is difficult to establish its origins properly. Very substantial arguments have been carried on in Germany for over 100 years about this key question: is this a medieval Christian site, or was it an old sacred Germanic site, used long before the Christian era began?

The distorted view of the Externsteine in the Hitler time
In the 19th century, the newly united nation of Germany consolidated itself; previously it had been a loose association of German speaking independent nation-states. And consequently the Externsteine was one site amongst many others, which was researched for a richer understanding of the historical development of the new nation.

However, as is well known, in Germany after World War One, German archaeology came under the influence of the national socialist movement and research was undertaken for nationalistic reasons, into old sites which could bolster the distorted view of Germanic culture and history, a view that the Nazis favoured. This was in the Hitler era, when all such old sites in Germany were tainted by National Socialism. Hence the Externsteine became a site associated for some decades with the debased cultic myths of the Third Reich. Some of the research done in this time, as part of the Nazi Institute for Germanic Archaeology, created in 1938, was done with the official patronage of SS chief Himmler. The focus of their research into the Externsteine was to prove that it had been established as the primary sacred centre for the Teutonic-Germanic tribes, to honour their pagan gods. There was a strong interest during the 1930-40's in proving that the Externsteine was a key site of the old Teutonic tribes.

This activity of some earlier generations of the present day Germans, has left a biased taint about it in the minds of many people. But these days we can objectively examine it, and the richly spiritual myths of the old Germanic peoples, without reference to any unhealthy ideas from the 1940's.

Some of the research carried out then did yield some information of value, but care has to be taken with it, as it was not honestly reported, and was also misconstrued to serve the propaganda purposes of the Third Reich.

The Celts and the Teutonic tribes
Before we consider whether the Externsteine was significant in the history of the Teutonic people, we need to consider briefly the relationship of the ancient Germanic tribes, or Teutonic peoples, to the Celts. We may think of the Celtic peoples as entirely separate from the Germanic (or Teutonic), but these two 'ethnic groups' were in fact extensively intermingled. From this joint stock come many of the European and British ethnicities of today.

The difference between the two groups is only slight. The Celts had more the tendency towards building of settlements or small towns and temples, whereas the old German people lived in scattered dwellings and were content with roughly hewn nature grottos. It is very likely that they worshipped the same gods, and were focused on the same nature deities and celestial influences.

In ancient times, around 3,000 BC, there were waves of people coming from the eastern boundaries of Europe, pushing westwards to Europe. They are known as the late Bronze Age

Urnfield culture. These people are widely regarded as the primal ancestors of what we now call the Celtic people. As these earlier peoples migrated further into Western Europe, they became partially assimilated into the indigenous Teutonic tribes.

So by about 2,000 BC, Western Europe was inhabited by what could be called Celtic-Germanic peoples, in the broadest sense. These two groups of people shared much in common with each other, in terms of customs and religious practises. Later on, at the time of the Roman invasion of Gaul, it became possible to identify specific Teutonic tribes.

The Teutonic people were more in the north, whereas the Celts were more in the south – however the religious activity of both groups was centred on the same deities, and interest in the same celestial influences, and nature spirits, etc. Furthermore, it could easily happen, in the changing flow of ethnic events, as these two groups fought for territory, that a site used by the Celts could late be used by the Teutonic people, and vice versa.

Since the Externsteine is situated in northern Germany, it is obviously the northern European Celts, even the 'Nordic' ones from lower Scandinavia, who were involved here. Certainly this group does include the ancestors of the present Germanic people, but it is also more comprehensive than this. As we shall see later, the spiritual significance of this sacred site derives from a **time before it is logically possible to speak of any ancestors of the present day Germans**. It goes back to a time before that particular segment of the old Celtic-Germanic peoples, who later became the German nation, had taken on a distinctive identity.

The spiritual beliefs of the Celtic people carried through into the time of the Teutonic people, whom the Romans encountered. These beliefs are presented in the beautiful and profound Norse myths as preserved in the old Icelandic language of the Edda. But these myths were created by the Celtic priests millennia ago. These were the priests of the ancient Celtic-Germanic peoples who arose as the Celts migrated into Europe and mingled with the indigenous tribes.

This absorption process lead to the forming of the widespread, and relatively uniform, Celtic-Germanic peoples of old Europe. Two millennia later the Teutonic tribes-people enter history. We shall show in this book that the Externsteine is certainly not a Church site dating back only to the Middle Ages. Nor is an old Teutonic site, with origins going not much further back than 300 BC. Rather it is an ancient Celtic site which arose from the ancient Celtic-Germanic peoples.

Medieval Church involvement & archaeological research
Let's start with a sketch of the historical background, as it is commonly understood. If it was not developed as a sacred site until the church purchased the land in the 12th century for ecclesiastical purposes, then our quest would end right here. But that is certainly not the case; it pre-dates the use made of it by the medieval church. There are brief medieval records from the Christian Church, which show that, as from the 11th century, it was used by the church as a place for contemplative monks, and for the holding of religious services. Until 1093 the site was owned by an old aristocratic family, in which year it was purchased by the Abdinghof monastery in Paderborn. The monks wished to make use of it for their religious activities; and a large relief carving was made on one of the rock towers.

The difficulty in discovering the great significance of the Externsteine is highlighted when we find that even the dating of this Christian inscription is disputed. Some art historians say that it dates to the 12th century, but others say it dates back to the Carolingian times, i.e., to the 9th century, which is the time of Charlemagne. To be able to examine the unique Christian relief carving, and determine when it really was carved and its veiled message, we need to firstly find out the age and origin of the man-made features of site itself. The source material about it is almost exclusively in German language books and articles.

Now, let's get an idea of the history from archaeological evidence, looking at the distinctive features, and then any indications as to their importance, from old historical documents. Firstly, we need to note that despite efforts from the National Socialists and also efforts from objective archaeological research undertaken by others, no evidence has ever been found of human usage, especially of habitation, at the Externsteine, earlier than medieval times.

The oldest ceramic fragments only go back as far as the 11th century; although there are also a few primitive tools dating from Stone Age times, ca 10,000 BC, but such tools will generally be found in the soil in Europe. Now, the primary point used by mainstream historians and religious scholars who wish to have it regarded as a Christian site, when they date this site, is that no artefacts from ancient times have ever been found by archaeologists. This point is encountered again and again, in virtually all the brief historical notes on the subject.

It is very important to note the fact that this argument is greatly overstated; it is not a crucial part of the discussion. The lack of evidence showing the presence of ancient peoples at megalithic sites is not uncommon at all. The argument that Celtic people did not establish the Externsteine as their sacred site, because there is no evidence of these people living there, is not a valid argument.

It is arguing from non-existent evidence, so to speak. For example at Stonehenge, the greatest Megalithic sacred site in the world, almost no items other than stone-working tools left by the builders, have ever been retrieved from all the archaeological research ever done there. As researchers have commented, it is as if a sign had been erected, 'No items to be left here'. And, once we understand the feeling for 'The Sacred' amongst earlier peoples, this is precisely what one would expect if the site were regarded as sacred.

We now know as regards Stonehenge, that the people did gather in large numbers, and did leave heaps of artefacts and rubbish behind them, but they left it all at a nearby place, at the present-day town of Durrington, not at Stonehenge itself. The people would proceed over to Stonehenge along a sacred causeway, for special ritual purposes, but no tainting of the sacred site occurred, as no mundane items were left there. Now this protocol is precisely the same with the ancient Teutonic tribes, as Prof. Wahle noted years ago in his Deutsche Vorzeit (German Prehistory), 'The holy places of these tribes were always sited at quite a distance from their habitations'. (2) So, the chance of any mundane artefacts being found there later on is very remote. Modern tourists may drop their soft-drink cans around such a place, but not the ancient tribes people!

In trying to establish the origin and hence the age of this amazing site, we can briefly note the statements of a geologist, a professor Andree, supervisor of the excavation work done in the Nazi era. He is widely viewed as having Nazi sympathies, and consequently as biased in his research work. It appears however, that he did discover a layer of sandstone scree in the layers of soil around Towers One to Three.

Scree is a term used for the rock fragments, and rough chips, that result when solid rock is cut into; and this happened here to make the several grottos inside the solid rock outcrops. Andree reported that this layer was located **under the layers** where medieval artefacts were discovered, and hence indicates that, prior to the medieval usage, it was an older culture that had hollowed out those grottoes in the Rock Tower One.

Nothing much else from the archaeological work done in the 1920's and 30's is worth considering, because the reports of such people were required to prove nationalistic theories about the cultural significance of the Teutonic tribes to modern Germany. So, what other evidence exists which may give a clue as to its origin? Since we are not seeking to establish a pre-conceived theory, and have no need to ensure that our assessments of the site establishes a Germanic origin, in the narrow sense, let's assess the features and see where they take us.

As we noted earlier, there are some burn marks on the walls of the grottos, that is, in the cavities hollowed out inside the rock towers. This is certainly evidence that sometime in the past people had lit fires in these grottos. The conservative theory had concluded that they were from the 12th century, at the time when the Church set up religious services there. But speculation had been around for a long time, from people outside the mainstream camp, that these might derive from ancient Celtic religious practises. So, in 2004 scientists from Heidelberg's Forschungsstelle für Achäometrie (Research Facility for Archaeometry) made a very careful analysis of samples of the rock, to determine the age of these burn marks, using a technique known as thermoluminescence analysis.

The results showed that some of these burn marks were from around 750 AD – long before Bishop Heinrich II took over the area for the church. Other fires date from perhaps as late as the 14th century. (3) So, the burn marks proved that the site was in use long before the church took it over, but did not go back into ancient Celtic times, nor even the more recent La Tené Celtic time (500BC- 100AD).

But as we shall see, they do point a finger at the damage done by Charlemagne. So the burn marks are a red herring in terms of ascertaining the original setting up of the site; we need to study the scanty historical reference made by Roman historians as they chronicled the wars between the Romans and the Teutonic tribes, in our quest to discover the purpose of the Externsteine.

Chapter Two: The Externsteine Weleda priestess and the Romans

Germanic links: the Teutoburger Forest, Caesar & the Weleda oracle

The Externsteine had an important role in the history of the Germanic tribes because it was in the Teutoburger Forest that a very major military conflict took place between the Roman Empire and the Teutonic tribes who were the ancestors, loosely speaking, of the present-day German nation. This event was the exceptional military triumph in 9 AD, by a small and improvised confederation of Germanic warriors, over three legions of the Roman Empire, lead by P. Quintilius Varus. This battle did not occur right outside the Externsteine. But it did occur in the Teutoburger Forest area – and thus not so far from the general area of the Externsteine site. For years a site near Detmold, which is only 10 kms from the Externsteine was regarded as probably the site of the battle. But in recent years another site near the northern end of the Teutoburger Forest, about 80 kms away to the north west, near the northern end of the Teutoburger Forest, has become favoured as the location of the battle.

This site is at Kalkriese Hill, which is 16 kms north of Osnabrück, here a large number of artefacts have been found, that are directly associated with a battle. See the colour-coded map for a clear view of the area. The bands of Teutonic warriors were far less in number than the Romans. They were hiding in the swampy thickets, ready to launch their surprise attack, but they were not equipped with the sophisticated weaponry of the Romans. The Teutonic tribes were lead by Hermann, from the Cherusci tribe, known to the Romans as Arminius (born 18? BC - died 19 AD). Hermann or Arminius had been brought up from childhood as a Roman citizen.

The Roman Empire had gained an uneasy control of Germania, the homeland of the Teutonic peoples. From his involvement with the Romans Arminius had gained experience in the art of war. In returning to his homeland, he found great discontent

18

amongst his people because of the autocratic rulership of the Roman administrator, Publuis Quinctilious Varus. He forged an alliance between the various (and often hostile) Teutonic tribes, and yearned to free his homeland from the invaders. His strategy was to lead the Roman troops into a dense forest, where the standard orderly formations of the legions could not be maintained.

He did this successfully and as the Roman troops became a disjointed line of soldiers, stretching over kilometres, the Germanic warriors attacked, and then proceeded to slaughter, some 20,000 Roman soldiers. No doubt the heavy armoury of the Roman soldiers was a hindrance to them in these circumstances. The battle lasted several days, and when it was over, the military victory of Arminius was truly remarkable. Three entire cohorts of Roman troops, and all their commanding officers, as well as auxiliary cohorts were all slaughtered. This was a unique achievement in military terms, because the Roman Empire had conquered all of Gaul with only eight legions. To lose three legions to a moderate size band of 'barbarian fighters' in this short battle created very great fear in Rome. It actually caused an exodus of people from the city, in case the 'barbarians' decided to launch an invasion of Italy.

A large metal statue, called the "Hermannsdenkmal" (Hermann's commemorative statue) commemorates this victory. Situated at a distance of approximately 7 km from Detmold, the monument is on top of a hill in the Teutoburger forest. The Roman historian Sueton reports that Octavianus Augustus Caesar, upon hearing of the defeat, tore his robe, let his hair and beard grow uncut for many months, and cried out in despair for the return of the legions. Historians have concluded that this event was possibly even a pivotal event in the pre-history of the later German nation, in so far as it assisted the German tribes to keep their culture and language, etc. So the question arises, what was the factor that spurred on these Teutonic fighters, to such an extraordinary act of defence of the homeland? Of course, one can say that it was just their wish to defend their homeland.

But the battle occurred in the general proximity of the Externsteine, although not in its immediate vicinity. And when an invading army threatens tribal lands, the priests or priestesses have of course, a key role in encouraging the warriors to defend their territory. And this is what happened in AD 9. As plans for repelling the Romans were being drawn up, the priestess at the Externsteine gave strong encouragement to the will of the fighters. This fact emerges from properly assessing indications from Roman historians about the role of the Externsteine priestess in regard to the Roman wars.

Rome was a terrible menace to the Externsteine priesthood in Teutonic times. We know this because already before the Varus slaughter, the Externsteine entered strongly into history, even if in a veiled way. Roman historians have left us with some tantalising indications of the influence of the Externsteine high priestess over the Teutonic tribes. It becomes clear they had a great concern about the threat of extermination of the Druidic priesthood by the Caesars.

The Roman military might and the seeress at the Externsteine

We can refer to the priests and priestesses of the Teutonic people, in general terms, as being akin to the Druids. The women were an integral part of the Celtic-Druidic religion of northern Europe. The Roman historian, Tacitus, reports that the Teutons respected their womenfolk, and in fact the leader of their religious life was a priestess. Tacitus reports that she was regarded as clairvoyant, and was called a 'Weleda', which is said by Tacitus to mean 'seeress'. He reports that knowing her pivotal importance, the Roman generals would seek to negotiate with this seeress. The wars between the Romans and the Teutonic people brought the high priestess into prominence, and no doubt gave her much prestige and power amongst the warriors.

Another Roman historian, Cassius Dio, in recounting the career of the Roman general Drusus, reports on an extraordinary incident, some years earlier, involving a Teutonic high priestess, which prevented the Roman troops from progressing further into the lands of the Teutonic peoples. Dio was one of the greatest historians of the ancient world, and a prominent Greek-Roman citizen. He was made a Senator, then a Consul, and later a Governor in Africa. As Dio reports, it happened in 9 BC, when a Roman Commander, Drusus, (stepson of Augustus Caesar) was attempting to march his legions ever further into Germany. This is only 18 years before the Teutoburger Forest battle. Drusus wanted to cross the Elbe River with his troops, but he was actually stopped by the appearance of an extraordinary Weleda.

A Weleda priestess of large size and very dramatic appearance, appeared in front of him and ordered him to go back, and dramatically prophesied that he would soon die. Cassius Dio reports:

> "Drusus undertook to cross this river (Elbe), but failing in the attempt, set up trophies and withdrew, {he failed} because a woman of superhuman size met him and said: "Whither, pray, art thou hastening, insatiable Drusus? It is not fated that thou shalt look upon all these lands. But depart; for the end alike of thy labours and of thy life is already at hand."

Cassius Dio goes on, commenting that,

> "It is indeed unbelievable that such a voice should have come to any man from the deity {the Weleda}, yet I cannot discredit the tale. For Drusus immediately departed, and as he was returning in haste, died on the way of some disease, before reaching the Rhine. And I find confirmation of the story in these incidents: just before his death wolves were prowling about the camp and howling; two youths were seen riding through the midst of the camp; a sound as of women lamenting was heard; and there were shooting stars in the sky. So much then for these events." (4)

Whether one chooses to accept all of this report, or to regard some of it as exaggerated, it shows the hypnotic power and charisma of the Weleda to the Romans, and therefore also to the Teutonic people at the time.

The priestess of the Teutoburger's 'Tall Towers' and General Ceralis

Now to return to Tacitus, he has a significant clue for our quest; we shall explore another event, this one took place 60 years after the Varus slaughter. Tacitus reports that the Weleda seeress still had a very high standing some decades after the Varus slaughter in AD 9. This woman by now would have been a successor of the one who encountered Drusus. This Weleda had prophesied another triumph over the Roman legions by the Germanic tribesmen, lead by another Teutonic warrior, called Civilis who had been given a position in the Roman army for some time. This battle became known as the Batavian insurrection, and it took place in 68-69 AD, when a group of Germanic warriors lead by Civilis, ambushed a Roman camp lead by General Ceralis, and overcame the Roman defenders. They then seized several Roman ships and sailed them away, going up the river Lippe. This river reaches up to the vicinity of the Teutoburger Forest.

Tacitus reports that the warriors then presented the main vessel, a Trireme, as a special war trophy, to the Weleda, their seeress "who lives in a high tower". Tacitus does not specify the Externsteine, but then no Roman official was ever allowed near this sacred site, so they had no definite knowledge of it. So, was it brought up to the Externsteine? Well, Tacitus also tells us that the Germanic tribes towed this vessel to her. After the river petered out, and the ship could no longer navigate the shallow waters, it had to be towed overland to the Weleda.

So the sacred site of these earlier Teutonic people in the report by Tacitus, need not be right next to a river, but also not too far from it either, and this is the case with the Externsteine. That the warriors may have towed the Roman trireme to the Externsteine in 69AD is quite reasonable, for two reasons. One is that this site lay near to a major trading route, a trail known as the 'Helle-way' (Helleweg), used for soldiers and trade for centuries already. So, there was a pathway leading through the dense forest. The other reason is that these tribes had a sacred ritual consisting of towing a boat along, on a cart. The cart contained an image of the Earth-goddess, called Nerthus. On the basis of this ritual, they could well have decided upon the tactic of towing the boat to their leader, on some form of improvised wagon. And to make use of this rite, now changed into a display of military insult to the enemy, would have been a potent cultural experience for the Teutons.

Significantly, Tacitus also tells us that the high-ranking Roman negotiators were not allowed to see the Weleda, but they understood that she lived in a "lofty tower". (5) Tacitus if he had known the actual site, would have said more accurately, that she officiated from "a tall tower". Tacitus does not say exactly where, beyond the headwaters of the Lippe River, that this "lofty tower" was located, and much discussion has arisen about this amongst German historians.

However, there are no high Celtic-Teutonic towers anywhere around the area where the Lippe arises, apart from a tower in the village of Kohlstädt, a few miles before the Externsteine, but this is a medieval monument. And the fact is that the Externsteine columns can indeed well be described as 'tall towers', formed by Nature. And, since the Teutons never constructed tall towers, it is certain from this reference alone, that the Externsteine is meant; namely the natural tall towers of rock where the seeress spent most of her day.

Taken together, all of these points provide a reasonable basis to conclude that the determination by the Teutonic tribes people to defend their homeland, and especially their religion from annihilation, was greatly strengthened by the priestess of the Externsteine. Just as the Externsteine priestess had been crucial in the military action of 9 BC against Drusus, and again in 69 AD against Ceralis, so too in 9 AD she would have encouraged the warriors to defend their territory against Varus. The priestess of this sacred site was in effect, exercising an influence that was a crucial factor in the emergence of the nation of Germany, many centuries later. It was at the sacred site of the Externsteine, the supreme spiritual centre of the Teutons, where the priestess with her retinue, carried out her duties, in the grottos and chambers of its tall sandstone towers.

Her influence radiating out from there, provided the cohesion and inspiration to the Teutons that defeated the might of Rome. So the motivation for the Weleda at Externsteine and her fellow priests, to urge the warriors to the fight, was a very urgent one. They were well aware of the extreme dangers posed to their Celtic-Germanic religious life by the Roman Caesars. Caesar Augustus had forbidden any Roman citizen from practising Druidism, and then Emperor Tiberius completely suppressed the Druids throughout the Roman Empire.

The Externsteine and the creation of a future German people

The Druids had established centers of learning throughout Gaul, and some of these sites would have had hundreds of acolytes in training. Some prominent French education towns of today were originally Druid sites of learning which the Romans had crushed, and then re-established as Roman centres of religious and civil learning; Narbonne for example was earlier the Druid 'college' of Narbo. There were many similar sites, such as those at Tolosa, Burdegela and Bibractis and at Alesia, now Saint Reine, just a short distance from Paris. This site was destroyed in 47 BC in the terrible and decisive battle between Gaius Julius Caesar and Vercingetorix. A few thousand acolytes would have perished or fled from the clashes with the Romans, who were intent of conquering Western Europe. Later in 54 AD Emperor Claudius ordered the full annihilation of the Druids.

It was said by Roman historians that the Druids carried out the cruel practise of sacrificing people to their gods at key seasonal or political times, and this included hanging or burning them. However, there is no independent confirmation of these statements, and bearing in mind the cruelty shown by the

Caesars in their campaign of cultural cleansing, and above all, their need to justify their aggressive campaign, such statements may be exaggerated or even baseless.

Victory over the Romans, specifically over Drusus, by the Teutonic warriors assembled in the Teutoburger Forest in AD 9, was vital for the survival of the culture and its religion. Many German people have quite reasonably concluded that the amazing victory by Arminius in the Varus slaughter was a significant factor in the creation of Germany. That is, it enabled the Teutonic tribes to develop their own Germanic culture, quite separate from the Latin world, and a thousand years later this lead to the precursor of today's Germany. As the Germans became part of Christendom, it would be in their own unique way. The great achievements of German mystics, scholars, theologians, writers, musicians and scientists made a valuable contribution to world civilisation.

However the Externsteine pre-dates these Teutonic people, being established long before these tribes are identifiable in the general mix of Celtic-Druidic-Germanic Europe. But it is clear that the Externsteine was used as a sacred place by the ancestors of the modern Germans at the time of the Roman wars, and therefore no doubt for some centuries prior to then. The Externsteine remained a central sacred site up until about 800 AD. It was at this time that the famous Christian conqueror Charlemagne attacked not only the Germanic tribes, but also specifically damaged the sacred images and chambers of the Externsteine itself.

Chapter Three: Charlemagne's campaign against The Externsteine

Charlemagne and his secret campaign

In the ninth century AD the Externsteine again had a role in a major confrontation between the Germanic tribes and a great power, this time the Holy Roman Emperor, called Charlemagne or Charles the Great. Charlemagne was discovering that the Germanic tribes were just as difficult for him to subdue, as they were for the Roman Caesars, 800 years earlier. The main war tactic of Charlemagne was as devastating as that of the Caesars, it could be described as, 'destroy their sacred sites, and you destroy the underlying force behind the Saxon tribes' resistance'. Although, in contrast to the sheer military ambition of the Caesars, Charlemagne was acting out of a sincerely held belief that it was his spiritual duty to enlarge Christendom. That Charlemagne carried out the attack on the Externsteine has never been clearly established, but we shall examine the evidence, and begin to see the full significance of the Externsteine.

When Charlemagne became the Holy Roman Emperor (742 - 814), after the death of his father Emperor Pepin, he became king of the Franks, and emperor of the greater part of European Christian world. But it was a large and unwieldy empire, and he spent his life engaged in military campaigns, to consolidate his empire and to also increase the number of Christian converts in the world. The Saxons, by now the predominant Germanic tribe, after having assimilated other smaller ones, were defending their territory with real vigour and caused major problems for Charlemagne. Little did he know that it would take 33 years of incessant fighting to bring this to an end, and even then he would never get a full victory. Hostilities ceased only through a compromise truce between the two sides.

The bitter conflict was triggered off in 772. In this year another raid by the Teutonic tribesmen on Frankish Christian outposts occurred, in which many priests and entire families of Christians were slaughtered. The Saxons were defending their territory and religious perspective, against people brought into their lands by the orders of Charlemagne. Charlemagne responded in a similarly aggressive manner. He mounted a military campaign, and forced the conversion of the Teutonic peoples to Christianity, on pain of death if they refused. Also large numbers of Saxons were deported to other parts of the Empire. Now, it is also reported in the Latin texts of the Imperial Frankish Annals that, as part of his reprisal measures, Charlemagne ordered the *beheading* of 4,500 Teutons at the town of Verden. And the report stipulates that this was carried out in a single day. However people who wish to uphold the noble image of Charlemagne, and who bear in mind his idealistic motivation for supporting Christianity, have queried this statement.

So what is the truth here? There may have been no slaughter at all. For it is a fact that the Latin verb for 'behead' (decollabat) is quite similar to the verb 'displaced' (delocabat), and so the scribe when copying original report into the official Annals may well have mixed these two words up.[2] So, the report probably said that in a single day the Emperor ordered that 4,500 Saxons **be re-located**, to be re-settled far away; and not 'beheaded'. A point in favour of rejecting the report of the atrocity is that no archaeological evidence of mass burials has ever been found at the place, which is now known as Verden.

There simply aren't any mass graves or skeletons there. But those who accept the report as accurate, reply that the relatives of the deceased may have taken all the bodies away to be buried elsewhere. And that is also possible, but it is not so likely to have been done so thoroughly as to leave no evidence at all. So the accusation has to remain a rumour, until definite evidence is found to either confirm or deny it.

In any event, it was in the same year 772 AD, that Charlemagne again set out for the general area of North Rhine-Westphalia, where the Saxons had many settlements; and this includes the Teutoburger Forest. Although this is not yet commonly agreed

---

[2] The Frankish Annals are on the Internet at http://en,.academic.ru/dic.nsf

by historians, it seems quite clear that Charlemagne's first priority was to destroy the primary sacred site of the Teutonic tribes, in an effort to undermine the religious values and attitudes that were providing them with their social cohesion. This was the first step in his military strategy. And this is where confusion arises, for the historical reports actually falsified the facts of his actions, for political-religious reasons. It is reported in various early medieval chronicles that in the campaign, various Saxon sites in this area were attacked, and that Charlemagne destroyed their forts and also their sacred carved columns, which were called an 'Irmin Column'.

This campaign included sites in the general area of the Externsteine, such as Iburg, and Eresberg. But a standard German history text will report that the most significant such attack occurred when Charlemagne stormed the Saxon settlement on a hill above Diemel River, called Eresburg (now known as Obermarsberg), which is 45 kms away from the Externsteine. We are also told that he stayed there for 2-3 days, to destroy its religious column. This standard historical viewpoint is based on what the Charlemagne's own historians, as recorded in the Imperial Frankish Annals, say about the life and campaigns of the emperor. The monks had been keeping brief historical chronicles for many years, but the number of monastic annals increased considerably in the reign of Charlemagne.

The historical Chronicles of Frankish Monasteries
Each monastery was to keep a chronicle of events, especially of events occurring in their vicinity. But since this was a task required of them by their emperor, and since the monasteries needed the good will of Charlemagne, they are not always objective. For example, in the official Frankish reports, the Saxons are described as treacherous and primitive people, whilst Charlemagne is hardly ever described as having a setback in his campaigns, and his intentions are always in the service of God. For example, with regard to precisely this campaign in the Teutoburger Forest area, a pious report from a Benedictine monastery at Lorsche, known as the Annales Laurissenses Maiores, is very

revealing. This report became part of the Frankish Imperial Annals. It was written soon after the events, and states:

> Karl conquered the stronghold of Aeresburg, and went up to the Irmin Column, destroyed the holy shrine itself and took away gold and silver, which he found there. And a severe drought prevailed at that time, so that there was a lack of drinking water at the place, where the Irmin column (had) stood, and the king wanted to remain there 2-3 days after the destruction of the sanctuary, but no one had any water to drink. However, as the army was resting, there streamed forth water, through divine Grace, in abundance, about midday, in a mountain torrent that no-one had known about, so that the entire army could drink their fill... (6)   (trans. edited by the author)

Now since Charlemagne was actually desecrating the greatest Celtic site in Europe during this campaign (see below), it is a directly political tactic to report that heavenly beings gave the emperor great moral support, by miraculously causing water to flow. Now, at this point, we need to examine briefly these reports, alert to the political 'spin-doctors' at work in them. As we start to examine the historical role of the Externsteine, we need to note some really significant facts. Firstly, no report exists in any Frankish historical document, of an attack ever being made by Charlemagne on the Externsteine!

So that is itself the real clue to a serious cover-up – because it is exactly this very site that the conqueror would want to attack! Secondly, the main report (above) focuses on the settlement of Eresberg, which was in fact, a fortified camp; it was not the primary sacred site of the Teutons. Thirdly, when Charlemagne had carried out the repression of the 'pagan' religion, it was his policy to set up Christian churches, bishoprics, and monasteries, giving them large tracts of land. In this way, since religion and the State were one, his imperial edicts could be communicated easily to the subjugated people through the church and they would be told that it was their religious and civil duty to obey.

This was done aplenty around Paderborn; in fact 5 years later, in 777, Charlemagne returned here and set up a residence for himself and his Court. We need to note here that Charlemagne was not motivated by a self-centred grab for power. He acted from an ideal, to raise the social life of the tribes dwelling in the forests of old Europe, up to a higher cultural standard. He actively sought out the best scholars and artists of the world, and invited them to establish an impetus for cultural renewal in his kingdom, centred on Aachen. (7)

Here the greatest library in Europe was created of this era, and also works of art and great churches were erected throughout his empire. But it was a religiously inspired ideal that was too dogmatic, and it was imposed on the Saxons in a fiercely militant way. It was here, not far from the Externsteine, that a formal ceremony was convened where the most powerful Saxon leaders were forced to swear loyalty to Christianity and to Charlemagne.

They were also required to hand over to the church a good residence and two small areas of arable land. The Germanic tribes were forced to accept Christianity under extreme pressure – it was either convert and forsake the old gods, or die. To conspire against the interests of the Emperor or the Christians, carried the death penalty. Now, even today historians are unclear about the Externsteine and its significance, and the inconsistencies in the above events. Lets examine the inconsistencies in the above report to find the underlying facts.

One: The Externsteine is never mentioned as being attacked, yet it is the central site for both their religious life, and for a sense of patriotism amongst the old Germanic tribes people.
Two: Charlemagne obviously set out to destroy the cohesiveness of the now unified tribes, but he is supposed to have done this by destroying the lesser Eresburg site.
Three: Since the Germanic-Saxon tribes were not a nation, they were separate tribes, united in defence of their common values,

so the destruction of any fortified settlement, which probably had a small Irmin Column, could not achieve Charlemagne's goal.

Four: The Externsteine with its sacred seeress is never mentioned, yet is by far the most significant Saxon sacred site. The destruction of the Externsteine is the only possible action which could impact across the tribal allegiances and possibly undermine the determination of the Germanic warriors.

Five: Divine intervention, in the form of a spring of water, gives supposed approval 'from on high' to the actions of the conqueror, silencing any critics in his own court (!).

Six: The report is written by a church person, dependent upon the Emperor, whose good-will is needed for the survival of the church

Charlemagne and the sanitized Frankish Chronicles

That Charlemagne did indeed attack the Externsteine, precisely because it was so socially significant a sacred site, becomes more obvious when we examine carefully other reports in the Frankish Imperial Annals (Annales regni Francorum), the official Frankish chronicle of events. One report indicates subtly that the Externsteine was involved, and yet it also keeps this fact under a veil:

> AD772 "Charlemagne conquered the {place called} Eresburg and reached the place which is called the Irmin column, and he set this place on fire." (8)

Now if we read this carefully, and bear in mind what we have learnt about the Externsteine as the key sacred site, then it becomes clear this statement is really saying:

> AD772 "Charlemagne conquered the {place called} Eresburg and (then continued on) and reached (the place) which is called the {place of the} Irmin column, and he set this place on fire."

In other words, Charlemagne first reached the place known as Eresburg, which is only a fortified settlement, and then went on and reached the second place, a place where the great Irmin Column was set up. The same shyness is found in the earlier report, the Annales Laurissenses Maiores. We can expand that report which we just read, in the same way. Here it is again,

> "Karl the Great conquered the stronghold of Aeresburg, and went as far as the Irmin Column, destroyed the holy shrine itself and took away gold and silver, which he found there…"

If we read this carefully, it also becomes a report telling discretely of two scenes of Frankish attacks:

> "Karl the Great conquered the **stronghold** of Eresburg, and {then) went {on} as far as {the place of} the Irmin Column, destroyed the **holy shrine** itself and took away gold and silver, which he found there…"

This report also is indicating that a <u>second</u> place of specific destruction is involved, because no capable chronicler would ever write that "the conqueror comes to a stronghold (the hill fortress), and conquers it, and then also continues further on and destroys a part of it" – i.e., of the same place! Especially as the first place has been described as a 'stronghold', whilst the second place is described as a 'holy shrine'. There was no holy shrine of any importance at Eresburg. It is obvious that a second site was attacked, for not even a clumsy writer would report on a campaign in which one place is conquered as if it were two places. Here it is clear that both reports are saying, in a veiled way, that in fact a second, quite separate, place was attacked, namely the Externsteine.

German scholars have detected this falsification of the reports. Already in 1835, Jacob Grimm detected inconsistencies with the Imperial Frankish Reports. One scholar of the campaigns of Charlemagne, F. Vater, notes how these two reports above give some detail about the attack on Eresburg, but virtually nothing about the events surrounding the destruction of the Irmin Column. (9) He also notes that a third chronicle, of the monastery of Amandi, reports in some detail of the Eresburg attack, but says nothing else about the campaign.

Now all this becomes quite intriguing when you know that there are two other contemporary chronicles from monks, which are also very discreet, but not as cunningly written as the above reports. They indicate the truth of the situation. The most significant here is the report in the Annales Moselani (the Mosel Annals), probably written by Richbod, a student of Alcuin, covering the years 703 to 798. But this chronicle is from an area towards the west of Germany, much further removed from the region of the Externsteine, than the other places from which we have reports. This report from the region of the Mosel River says:

> "Emperor Karl went to war in Saxony and destroyed its holy shrine, which was called the Irmin Column."
> (8)

So, there we have it, as honestly as we can find in the old chronicles. The supreme holy shrine of all the Teutonic peoples was severely damaged, and therefore we may safely conclude, this was the primary aim of the invasion. And, as a further indication of this situation, there is the Annale Petaviani (Petavian Annals), which reports:

> "Emperor Karl pushed further towards Saxony, conquered the Eresburg, {then} reached as far as the {other} place which is called the {place of the} Irmin Column, and set that place on fire." (8)

In other words, here is a truthful report. We have in fact two separate events, and two separate places. So, summing all this up: a stronghold is conquered (not destroyed), then a holy shrine is destroyed, indeed partly by being set on fire. The holy shrine is not the place called 'Eresburg', for that was a fortified settlement on a hill. That cannot be compared with a place as special as the Externsteine, which had already been a sacred site for these people for about 1,000 years. So, the other place has to be the Externsteine, for it is indeed a holy shrine, and it is this which is called the (place of) the 'Irmin column'. It is the great sacred column at this place that Charlemagne then sets on fire. Remember the burn marks we mentioned earlier, found in the grottos, which were scientifically examined? They were dated to the medieval times; and some dated to early medieval times. As the scientists who undertook the research, report, one is dated to approximately 735 AD, another to 680 AD. There are others which could not be dated – but these may well date from 772, because the margin of error is around 50 years.[3] So some of these burn marks on the walls could well be a remnant of the arson and pillaging by Charlemagne!

That is why the Charlemagne spent 2 to 3 days at 'the place of the Irmin Column', which he sets on fire. Now the Irmin Column was made of wood, and no doubt was quite tall, but a large contingent of soldiers does not need 3 days to cut it down. So during this time Charlemagne was overseeing the destruction of the Externsteine complex. Scholars are aware that the site of 'the place of the Irmin Column' could indeed have been the Externsteine itself. There is no historical reason to invalidate this possibility, but because of the false reports about this event, the Eresburg is still often suggested as the site of the attack by Charlemagne. We also note that an English 9th century historical record, reports that Charlemagne lost many of valued fighters in this military campaign in 772,

> In the year 772, Charles, the king of the Franks, having collected a powerful army and assembled the warlike forces of his kingdom, invaded the nation of the Saxons, and after having lost many of his principal and most noble men betook himself home.[4]

----

[3] Robin Jähne, writing in *Licht in das Dunkel der Vergangenheit*, p. 88-89
4 The Annals of Roger de Hoveden for 772, in The History of England and of   Other Countries of Europe, trans. H. Riley, H. Bohn, London, 1853.

34

So it was a military campaign vehemently opposed by the Saxons; the question is whether this fierce resistance was encountered at the Eresberg fort, or at the Externsteine. There are several other outstanding points which these two reports together manifest.

The historical chronicles show the pivotal power of the Externsteine

One: As we have noted, the Externsteine is never mentioned at all, in either report, and yet it is the most obvious and the most crucial site for him to attack.

Two: Yet some reports do make it clear that Charlemagne attacked a second site; and this was the place where the great Irmin Column was set up.

Three: The report from Mosel tells us that the central sacred shrine of the Saxons was destroyed and thereby implies that this was the key reason for the campaign.

Four: The Externsteine has been attacked! The ruined state of its features show this; the damage is due to brute force, not the weather. It was attacked in a very determined and thorough way; which would take 2 or 3 days to carry out.

Five: In fact, as the direct aftermath of this attack, a huge Christian relief, of a Carolingian type was carved into the main rock outcrop! This type of art is named after the artwork developed in Charlemagne's reign (Charlemagne was called Carolus Magnus, in Latin), he would have ordered the carving to be done.

Six: This act of carving a core Christian scene here, very boldly imposed a Christian message onto the most sacred site of the entire Teutonic world.

Seven: This Christian scene strikingly depicts a Christian saint standing on a bent and disempowered symbol of the Celtic religion! (see next section). An unmistakeably contextualised religious-political statement!

Eight: Charlemagne's sacrilegious actions against the Externsteine did not cower the Germanic tribes, but on the contrary impelled them to an even more vehement unified rebellion. Their intense outrage resulted in a much more fierce military campaign against Charlemagne; it lead to Wittekind's lethal resistance movement. Wittekind set up a fierce warfare against the Franks which lasted 33 years, until 804 AD.

It is for these reasons that one can conclude that Charlemagne did attack the Externsteine, but the chronicle writers decided to omit or veil this inflammatory, not to mention criminal, action from the official record. The technique of falsifying history, especially after the victor has carried out illegal actions, is of course a common fact of political life. This is the key point to understand, if you are interested in the history and significance of this site, and why the mainstream historians are reluctant to make a link between the Externsteine and Charlemagne. The reason his actions caused such intense anger, and the reason that the records are deceptive, is that the Externsteine was the primary sacred site of these people. So there would have been here not just any symbolic column (called an Irmin column; see next section), but a very large and important one.

For, as we have seen, the Externsteine was the central sacred site for the Teutonic peoples from Roman times. But this is not when it began to be used. It has had a very long history indeed, and there would have been phases of development ever since it was established. It may well be the case that it was about 3,000-2,700 BC that the Externsteine was first developed in its initial, simple features. This is in same time-frame in which so many sites and cultural activity were constructed, or began, such as the Great Pyramid and the Sphinx, Stonehenge, and the Newgrange chamber in Ireland.

So summing up, we can say that in early medieval times, the Externsteine was the most sacred and most politically significant site in the Celtic-Germanic world. It thus represented a threat to the determination of Charlemagne to impose Christianity as a state religion on these people. We understand now why the involvement of Charlemagne with the Externsteine was 'swept under the carpet'. It is also true that Christendom would bring many profound and uplifting ideas about ethics and divine beings and specifically Christian sacred truths, into their culture. But if Charlemagne had found it possible to persuade the Saxons through trade and commerce, and a less harsh military campaign, less suffering would have been endured by the Saxons, and the Externsteine would have survived intact.

We can now explore just what it was that made the Externsteine site so potent, so awe-inspiring to the Celtic-Germanic people. What were the spiritual truths, which are depicted in its strange figures and forms? And what was the religious life that the site was meant to nurture? After we have explored these questions, we shall also take note of the remarkable Christian carving, to see what its significance is.

Chapter Four: the old Celtic people and their religion

The Nordic-Teutonic worldview in the Edda

To understand the Externsteine in its various phases as an ancient Celtic site, we need to know something of the worldview of the ancient Celts. The only texts that teach this are from the later Germanic tribes, the descendants of these ancient Celts of northern and western Europe. We can say that the religious and spiritual views of the ancient Celts and the later Teutonic peoples were very similar. The texts that preserve the teachings of the later Germanic people are preserved in versions written in Icelandic. These texts are called 'the Edda', they were written down in the 13th century.

We can be grateful to the unknown scholar who at that time painstakingly preserved all he could of these ancient pre-Christian texts. In evocative language, the Edda tells of the gods and primordial beings involved in the creation of world and of humanity, and of the subsequent entry of evil beings into the scheme of things. The various texts that make up the Edda deal with profound cosmological questions in simple, but beautifully vivid, language.

It tells of the arising of the planet Earth out of a vast primordial 'Earth-human', called Ymir, who is like the Adam Kadmon of mystical Hebrew teachings. That is, Ymir was in effect that primal human who was the earth itself, on some kind of soul level; his soul was the soul of all the Earth. So Ymir contained all the animals and human beings in his (or rather, its) consciousness. In later ages these all start to separate out, and appear as specific species on the Earth.

Let's hear about how Creation is described in the Edda, in a translation that will attempt to gives us the actual images and thought-sequence of the original Icelandic text, as closely as possible. The Edda creation stories start with the emergence of the what we call the cosmos on some non-physical level of being, that is, with a cosmos that is not yet composed of matter. From the Song of the Seeress or *the Voluspa* we read,

> It was at the beginning of the Ages [5]
> when Ymir made habitation.
> sand was not there, nor sea, nor cool waves;
> nothing of the Earth was to be found,
> nor of the firmament.
> An abyss there was – deep, wide voids –
> but grass, nowhere.   (author's translation) (9)

This verse presents some remarkable and vividly graphic ideas. It appears likely from the first line, that time itself was regarded not as a simple, linear thing, but a series of Ages, if so, this was a feature to be found in many earlier cultures.[6] It also tells us that the primordial Earth had its beginning at the commencement of time, but in the form not of a physical planet, but as something metaphorically described as the giant Yymir. Gradually, from Ymir all the current realms of nature emerged. So, Ymir is a metaphor for a unified primordial Earth. But even more intriguing, Ymir represents the unified Earth on a soul level, rather than a material level, because matter did not yet exist at this remote time.

So when Ymir is mentioned, the Edda is referring to the many consciousness units or 'souls' of the animal and human realms collectively, as well the elves, dwarves and giants, etc, that in their religion constituted this primordial Earth. A similar view

---

[5] It is more poetic to render line 1 as "Young were the years" or "It was at the beginning of time" as does C. Larrington in her valuable work "The Poetic Edda" and Bandle et.al. in "The Nordic Languages". Or as, "Urzeit war es…" [the primordial Age it was] or "Einst war das Alter…" [once upon a time] as does Genzmer, and Simrock, respectively, but in my rendering I have tried to get closer to the imagery of the original.

[6] The Icelandic noun, alda, is in the plural and means either plural Ages or plurality of human beings. Thus, the alternative is, it was at the beginning of humanity's existence. Most scholars take it as referring to the Ages, even if they then make 'the Ages' into the customary singular, 'Age'.

that Creation derived from a non-physical state of being and gradually condensed into matter is to be found in other ancient myths; it is not unique to the Edda. It is found in various creation myths, and in profound texts of ancient religions.[7]

The main focus of the above verse is the Abyss, which is described as a potent gap, apparently consisting of deep or wide voids.[8] This abyss seems to be a kind of receptacle waiting for its many inner spaces to be filled. The creative influences from beyond the Earth, stream into this. So, at this first epoch of time, the sun and the moon have not yet been formed, but giants and ranks of high spirit beings inhabit the primordial world. In the place where one should expect to find the Earth, there was only this deep wide abyss.

Together all these realms formed the great Tree of Life, called Yggdrasil, which has nine realms. Furthermore, we are told in the text called The Gylfaginning, in the Younger Edda, how twelve streams of creative power ray into the deep abyss. These arise streams from the "Well of Hvergelmir". (10) Elsewhere in the Edda, this 12-fold stream is very significantly called The Eliwagar, meaning 'the foreign waves'; that is they are not terrestrial. Moreover we are told that Eliwagar emerged from the Well of Hvergelmir, which is situated in the mysterious icy realm of Nifelheim, which existed long before the Earth was created,

> "Many ages before the Earth was made", said Jafnhar, "was Nifelheim formed, in the midst of which lies the well, Hvergelmir. From this well flow the twelve rivers..." (11)

---

[7] It is also part of ancient religions, such as Babylonian, and Indian, and of 19th century spiritual movements such as the Theosophical Society, and is described in detail in the writings of the Goethe scholar Rudolf Steiner.
[8] The noun here, 'ginnunga', is actually of unknown origin and meaning, despite several ingenious interpretations. However it is very reasonably rendered as 'yawning abyss', thus tautologically reinforcing the earlier word for abyss. Although it is usually considered singular here, it is in the plural, being a 'plural nominal'; but it can be considered as plural, if this enhances the intended idea.

So in the Edda, creation actually commences with a non-physical realm, from which matter gradually condenses. And since the number twelve is a zodiacal number, mentioned in ancient Babylonian writings of 4,000 years ago, it appears that here the ancient Celtic priests were referring to a belief in subtle influences coming from the twelve zodiac constellations. In effect the Edda is saying that the metamorphosing of this primordial unified Earth 'soul', Ymir, into the many and varied life forms it gradually developed, was due to the in-raying zodiacal influences. Since the word Eliwagar means 'foreign waves', it appears that these twelve streams derive from beyond the Earth, from the cosmos.

So presumably they were thought of as energies streaming in and moulding this primordial earth 'entity' from the stars.[9] This zodiacal factor appears to apply because the Edda also specifies that there are twelve gods, and gives the names of their twelve realms; even though in fact the number of deities mentioned in the various texts is a little more than twelve. In addition it is noteworthy that the Edda specifies that their goddesses were to be equally venerated as the gods; not surprising for a people who placed their 'Weleda' seeress at the top of their religious hierarchy. (12)

So the tribes-people around the Externsteine and indeed throughout the Germanic-Celtic lands, lived with this vibrant picture of creation, wherein spirit beings from the zodiacal stars created the Earth by utilizing the vastness of Ymir's energies and substances. And all of this was achieved by the actions of many gods or goddesses, and also lesser spirits, such as elves and gnomes and giants. This belief of the old Celts in the existence of many spiritual beings and strange energies in nature, and the intimate interconnectedness of humanity to nature, was a really vibrant one.

---

[9] Although the Eliwagar proceeds from the Well of Hvergelmir, which is a cool misty realm, this appears to be not the point of origin of these streams, but only their secondary location from within the terrestrial sphere, of the four elements.

To understand the Externsteine in its context, we should note the fact mentioned earlier, that the spiritual perception which underlies the ancient Celtic people was absorbed by the later Celts and the Teutonic tribes. Thus it was spread across all of central and northern Europe (Gaul and Germania), as well as Scandinavia; it was nurtured amongst these Celtic and Teutonic peoples. A primary source of their beliefs was, in all probability, the priesthood centred on the Externsteine.

There exists a very old early German poem, called the Wessobrunner Prayer, dating from about 800 AD, which comes from Bavaria, in southern Germany. So it was written down in the Carolingian period, the time of Charlemagne, when the tribes-people were still being converted by Christian missionaries. This prayer contains a passage very similar to this creation account in the Edda, but it is now part of a Christian text, so it ends with a prayer to Almighty God,

> This I learned from mortal men,
> as the most marvellous wonder,
> That the Earth was not, nor the Firmament,
> Nor tree nor mountain were,
> That not even a star (?) was,
> nor did the sun shine,
> nor did the moon gleam,
> nor {was there} the sea, so glorious.
> But when nothing was of endings or limits,
> there was the one almighty God.........   (13)

One can see how very close is this text, from far away in southern Germany, to the Voluspa from northern Europe and Iceland. The same kind of cosmogony is at present here; it lingered on for centuries into the Christian era. The old Celtic teachings existed throughout long ages across north and central Europe, and the teachings were communicated to the local people in the form of myths and verses. These were recited from memory down through the generations. So the composer of the Wessobrunner Prayer presents his view of creation, interwoven with the age-old Celtic knowledge, which he probably heard from the elders in the community. He sees no reason to isolate this from his newly adopted Christian convictions.

The Edda also has a section about the entry of evil into creation, in the guise of a fallen god called Loki, who was helped by his host of 'dark elves'. Through the myth of the death of Baldur, the Edda then focuses upon the effect on the consciousness of human beings of Loki; the arising of evil tendencies in the human being. The Edda in dealing with this difficult theme, makes the profound theological point that the highest of the gods, Odhin or Wuotan – the supreme deity in the Nordic myths – at a certain point in the past, has to specifically order that a place is made available at the table of the gods in the great hall of Asgard, so that Loki can have a place there. Only then can Loki start to trigger off events which bring about moral problems, and then eventually, the departure of the gods from human consciousness. This is described as a tragic phase of human history, the Twilight of the Gods.

This situation, wherein the gods are departing from human perception, and evil is becoming a human trait, is described as especially sad by the Edda. This tragic aspect is told through the story of the death of the radiant god Balder. The Icelandic texts about the death of Baldur are a poignant contemplation on the tragic inroads into society made by evil; it is a kind of Celtic version of Paradise Lost. The Edda takes on a kind of apocalyptic quality through the potent images about the battle between good and evil power, recorded in the Song of the Seeress. There are quite deep implications here about the meaning of life, and ethics, and the future of humanity on the Earth.

The art of the Celtic people, their burial sites and sacred places also indicate that to these people, the divine and the evil spirit beings in the Edda were very real. To the Celts, it was as if the natural world was alive with various spirit beings and subtle energies; changing with the seasons. And these energies were interlinked with forces streaming in from the moon, the sun and the stars.

The many-layered cosmos of the ancient Celts
Their worldview was, in common with other earlier peoples, a vibrantly spiritual one, with different realms of planes of existence for the various spirit beings. It is described in the Edda as consisting of nine realms. The exact categorizing of these nine realms on the Tree of Life is difficult today, as the various realms mentioned in the Edda are not precisely identified. For example, it is hard to know whether a realm has more than one name, or whether two different realms are being mentioned. But in general it appears that the cosmos of the old Celtic and the later Teutonic peoples consisted of Midgard, the realm where people live, which we might call the physical world. Then, subtly influencing this, our world, was a realm called Alfheimr, inhabited by good, radiant, nature spirits called 'light elves'.

Associated with this, perhaps symbiotically near to it, is a warm fiery realm called Muspelheim. From here destructively fiery beings could arise and affect Midgard. This was especially predicted to happen at Ragnarok, the time when an apocalyptic battle between good and evil would occur. As a polar opposite to these bright, fiery realms is the somewhat sinister, murky and cooler realm of Swartalfheimr, where dwelt the dark elves. And there is also a realm called called Nifelheimr, with similar qualities to Swartalfheimr, again symbiotically near to it. This is a primordial realm of cool darkness, but inwardly filled with creative potential, for matter is to form out of this somewhat un-spiritual, murky realm.

But in indicating this womb of matter as something ignoble, the Celtic worldview here has a nuance that is common to other spiritual teachings. For the nuance here is similar to a Gnostic one, in so far as the Gnostics also considered matter to be a lowly, dubious thing. It is in this realm that the fountain Hvergelmir exists, as we noted earlier. It is from this fountain that the creation of our material planet derives. From this realm the Earth had been condensed down into physical reality at the beginning of the Ages of time.

The noble gods are called the Aesir, and they dwelt high up in the radiant realm of Asgard. Now, it is very likely that the Externsteine was regarded as the physical representative of Asgard, and was considered somehow a kind of doorway to the real Asgard – and this would have been a major reason for the sacredness of this site. The greatest of the gods in Asgard is called Odhin. But there is also another rank of high deities, called the Vanir, who are only briefly referred to in the Edda, they dwell in Vanaheimr. Near to the Earth was the realm of Jotunheimr where the giants dwelt, many of whom were hostile to the good intentions of the gods. Finally, below the Earth was the realm of the dead, known as Helgardhr. The myths of the old Teutonic priests instructed the people about these beings and their role in the life of the tribe.

It is obvious from sociological studies and familiarity with ancient myths from many cultures that, in ancient times interest in spiritual experiences and interaction with spiritual beings was very deep; indeed it was a core part of life. Since we humans naturally incline towards whatever speaks to us the most persuasively, it is a reasonable conclusion that, in ancient times people built these sites because such spiritual things were very real to them. Just as a lot of modern societies naturally incline to technology and sport, ancient peoples were endowed with a natural awareness of the spiritual side of creation, and so they were inclined towards that. Hence the interest of earlier humanity in building sacred sites through which they could try to have interaction with this spiritual reality.

The high priests or priestesses were regarded by the tribes people as persons who had developed this awareness to an enhanced degree, and could assist others to do likewise. They were also in a position to provide ethical instruction and guidance as to the will of the spiritual beings that they believed they experienced through their inner experiences. To do this in an effective way, and to honour the sacred energies that they felt, they built their special sites.

The key to understanding the design of ancient sacred sites is to keep in mind that such topics as the after-life, the influence of gods and goddesses, of nature spirits and of planetary and zodiac energies in the seasons, were the usual focus of ancient humanity. People were different to us, in earlier ages. Their view of life was really imbued with a sense of otherworldly energies and beings. It is important to realize that all ancient cultures had a perception of the spiritual, as a prominent element of their existence. So the spiritual was the core element of their cultural sites.

One of the results of this openness to spiritual realities was their natural inclination to incorporate this fully into daily life. It also produced a feeling of how sacred these higher realities are, and how important it was to develop the right relation to them. In earlier times the entire social structure could be based on ensuring that people were attuned to the will of spiritual beings (the gods), or the power of various spiritual energies. Now, all of this is still puzzling to most people in western civilisations. But it was not so long ago that western culture itself had some remnants of practises designed to keep society in harmony with the unseen world.

Ancient nature-spirituality and modern humanism
Remember the old-fashioned children's toy, the 'jack in the box'? It was a box that, when you open it, has a nasty little face on a spring which then flies up. As Nancy Arrowsmith points out, a few hundred years ago people in Europe became evermore aware of how much of the wonderful old forests had been relentlessly cut down. They sensed that many of the nature-spirits who used to dwell in the great forests were now seeking a refuge. This was because they had lost their homes amongst the trees, as a result of the de-afforestation process. So people made a special little box with a lid, which was kept in a quiet corner in their house, to be set aside as the dwelling place of the tree or bush spirit.

But to ensure that their children did not displease the little sprite whose new home was inside this box in their house, they made a duplicate of this special little box, and put inside it an ugly face, attached to a spring, and then they told the child to open it up. The child received thereby a rude shock, and consequently stayed away from the real home of the tree-sprite. From this lesson in the etiquette of how to live with 'nature spirits', came the ill-advised 'toy' called a jack in the box – once the reason for the contraption had been forgotten! (14)

We often relegate to children what was once a serious concern of adults in their interaction with the transcendent. The Halloween pumpkin masks have their origin in this, they were once serious forms, designed to help Celtic peoples against demons which they believed gained strength in the autumnal days as the sun-forces weakened. Not only is our modern mindset remote from the nature spirituality of the old Celts, but also, some religious institutions in our culture have at times appropriated and distorted this material. An example of such behaviour by religious authorities in Europe can be found in regard to the 'trolls'.

These supposedly fierce, evil nature spirits of Norway, (which are also reported in the folklore literature, from Iceland, Finland and the Faeroe islands), are known to Christian children today as evil beings, through such tales as 'The Billy Goats Gruff'. However, these were originally regarded as harmless faeries to the Scandinavian people. The term 'troll' (or Thusser, in Norwegian) became categorized as evil and violent during late medieval times. This occurred as Christian churches struggled to win the loyalty of the Norwegians, to whom these beings were especially important and real. A collection of old Scandinavian fairy tales can in fact reflect this sociological process, by having stories depicting all trolls (or Thusser) as good, and another story depicting them as evil.[10]

A process of vilification has been clearly undertaken, for the original Thusser were described as nature-spirits similar to the

---

[10] One such rare work, from ca.1880 is "The Yuletide Stories of the North; fireside tales of Sweden, Norway, Denmark and north Germany", edit/trans., Benjamin Thorpe Simpkin, Marshall, Hamliton, Kent & Co. Glasgow.

'elf' of British folklore. It is said that they dwelt inside mysterious mounds, and earth-barrows with their herds of tiny animals and busied themselves with harmless agrarian activities. They were averse to sunlight, but this is a quality they have in common with the reports about many types of Faeries.[11] To the Church, such beings as these were seen as competition to their deity, so their influence had to be countered.

It is clear that this holistic sense of the spiritual had another aspect to it; it was the quest to directly know these lofty realms and beings, and to directly experience the subtle seasonal or celestial energies associated with them. This search was also referred to as the quest for 'initiation'. The meaning of the term initiation varies widely from culture to culture, but on a mystical level, it refers to a process that gives a kind of spiritual re-birth to the acolyte and the ability to know the will of the gods of that culture. Consequently, most ancient societies had a mystical religious system for finding a pathway into the spiritual reality, through 'initiation'. It is clearly the case that the Externsteine was just such a site.

We can gain a good idea of just how alive with spirit beings Nature was to these very early Celts, through the folklore of the northern and western Celtic-Germanic peoples, who are their descendants. And the folklore of these later peoples is very much focussed on the world of elves, dwarves, giants and gods. Fragments of their folklore survived into the early Middle Ages. We can be grateful that in the 19th century, scholars such as Wilhelm Mannhardt and Jacob Grimm undertook valuable work in this field, compiling what remained of the nature folklore of these people. From these we learn for example, that the Celtic-Germanic people considered that each tree had a sprite or fairy living in it. Moreover, in some trees there dwelt a guardian spirit being, who protected each person, or even the entire tribe.

---

[11] Nancy Arrowsmith, A Field Guide to the Little People, London: Pan, 1977, page 110.

48

This tree spirit helped the people in various ways, and once the tree was identified, it was sacrosanct, and could never be harmed. Some northern tribes always kept a small grove of sacred trees, not too distant from their dwelling, in which was located the special tree. And moreover the rocks and other geological features were often experienced as permeated by spiritual energies. An 11th century report from the German state of Hesse, tells of the' witte wîwer' or 'white women' who dwelt in the large stone clumps, or amongst tree roots.

Clad in coarse green clothing, they could be seen rising up into the air, on moonlit nights, their long hair streaming out behind them. On certain mountain tops it was said, one can see the imprint of their hands and feet in the rock or the ground. Further to the west of Germany, in the Eifel district, similar beings dwelt in rock grottoes, and if they were driven away, by changed natural circumstances or through the actions of the Christian clergy, then the land could lose its fertility or the trees in the vicinity could wither. (15) So how do the beliefs of the old Celtic-Teutonic people manifest at the Externsteine?

Sacred rocks, Externsteine and Chief Seattle
At this point we need to note again that the Externsteine consists of a number of huge rock towers, which have quite a potent ambience about them. But, it is the case that prominent rocks were often a central part of ancient peoples holistic spirituality. It is useful here to look at the famous American document, the 'Speech of Chief Seattle'. The speech was made in 1856, as a response to the demands from the American government that the indigenous people depart into 'reservations'.

A careful academic study revealed that Seattle's original speech, about how livingly interwoven were his people to the land, included a reference to ancestral 'memory rocks'. However when the text was published on posters and elsewhere, a mystical reference made by Chief Seattle to the rocks in the landscape was deleted. His reference was probably considered meaningless to modern readers. (The popular poster based on Chief Seattle's speech contains many sections that were never part of the great Chief's speech.)

Furthermore, even when these words are included in the authentic translations of Seattle's speech (from his native Suquamish), these conscientious, modern scholars really struggle to find an appropriate, meaningful clause. Their translations report Chief Seattle as saying in this connection:

> "Even the dumb rocks...*thrill with memories* of past events connected with the fate of my people."

or, in a more carefully researched translation;

> "Even those unspeaking stones....*are loud with the events and memories* of my people...."[12]

But even these careful modern translations are still baffling to us today. Just what is it that these earlier people felt was so special about large rocks? These translations tend to suggest that, because rocks are so long lasting, they easily become a metaphor for the long history of a tribe. But that is not quite what the Chief was saying.

The meaning here from Chief Seattle, and in the other similar accounts, is not about a museum archive or a symbol, rather it appears to be that of an active *resounding* or a living resonance. That is, the rock livingly resonates to the holistic mind-set of earlier peoples, delivering images or intense emotions from somewhere back in the history of the tribe, to the mind of the priests or elders of the tribe. In effect, Chief Seattle was saying;

> "*Even those unspeaking rocks...resonate with the events and memories of my people.*"

It seems that to the consciousness of older cultures, highly significant events in the life of a tribe were 'stored' somehow, in rocks. And, the Externsteine is after all, a series of huge rocks! Even to us modern tourists, the Externsteine rock towers are amongst the most potently atmospheric of any sacred site in the

---

[12] Chief Seattle's speech in, 1st : the version by Dr. Henry Smith, and 2nd : the version by Prof. William Arrowsmith, How Can One Sell The Air? 21, 75.

world; how much more potent they would have been to the holistic feelings of the old Celts! It is interesting here to note that in central Australia is the famous Ayres Rock, or "Uluru".

The indigenous people in that country are deeply offended if tourists walk up onto it. Because to the Aborigines, it is a kind of doorway into spiritual realities; it 'speaks' about events and beings in spirit realms. This is an attitude almost totally incomprehensible to the non-indigenous people.

It is very likely that the ancient Celts had a similar attitude to these great rock towers. We have noted earlier that the rock columns of the Externsteine have, or seem to have, a number of strange figures carved on them. They also seem to have been shaped on their sides, so as to create various odd faces in profile.

The most prominent of these is the figure of a very large entity that seems to be hanging or suspended, see illustration 3. This figure was very likely created by deliberate intent, by making use of a partial outline of this shape that had already been formed accidentally by cracks in the large rock wall. It is a theme of the Edda that their foremost deity, Odhin, was involved in special spiritual processes in the attempt to gain wisdom to help humanity.

To undertake these called for courage and selflessness, and also involved suffering and effort. This is reported in one of the most esoteric of the Eddic texts, called "Odhin's Runes-song', incorporated in a text called Runatal. Here it is recounted how Odhin travelled to the fountain where the mysterious Urd was seated.

Odhin is in search of the 'runes', and to do this, he must travel to Urd's fountain. Urd is one of the three 'Fates'; she is the one who gazes back into the past. The runes are the magical signs, which contain the key to higher spiritual knowledge. Perhaps it is more correct to say that the runes opened the pathway to the priests that helped them in acquiring higher knowledge.

3   Odhin on the Tree of Life. Natural clefts in the rock been enhanced to depict Odhin hanging from Yggdrasil, the Tree of Life.

The Edda and Odhin's sacrifice

It appears that this includes the ability to know the course of evolution charted out by the gods for humanity. Odhin recounts his experience in 'Odhin's Runes-song':

> ….I know that I hung on a windy Tree nine nights long;
> wounded by the spear, consecrated to Odhin,
> I myself consecrated to myself:
> on that tree of which
> no one knows from what root it grows.
> They gave me neither food nor drink,
> I lowered myself down, took up the runes,
> groaning I took them up, then fell I to the earth….
> spiritually I grew and I thrived;
> wise became I.
> From a word unto word was I lead to word;
> from deed unto deed was I lead to deed.

(Author's trans.)

The huge figure carved into the rock outcrop is surely Odhin, depicted during his great ordeal. And the above text explains what is happening in this event. The text here however, is seldom commented on because it is so obscure; its obscurity comes from its other-worldly spiritual-religious implications. Let's see if we can get clarity about this verse from the Edda, to properly understand and appreciate the prominent feature here. Firstly, the priests or priestesses of these people probably did not just make pronouncements to their people from their hunches. As the religious leaders they would have been required to undergo a spiritual development process, some form of ordeal and testing. This was, and indeed still is, the case in shamanistic cultures across the world, such as those in South America and the Far East. These cultures are an approximate modern counterpart to the old Druidic system.

The above verse also poses the great riddle as to why Odhin, the foremost of the gods, would need to get wisdom. It tells us that Odhin sought to access the runes **specifically in order to guide** the Celtic-Germanic peoples. One reason that the help of Odhin was needed was that through the actions of the evil god Loki, evil had come into human existence. So Odhin underwent a sacrifice to gain the wisdom to help humanity, as a counterbalance to the power of evil beings.

But still the question remains, just why would a god need to get wisdom, or be consecrated unto himself? The answer can be found in the idea of a priest who becomes a vessel of the tribal deity. This concept was quite widespread in the ancient world, and presumably also amongst the Nordic-Germanic people. It means a person who becomes the vessel for a deity, and who is often given that deity's name. It is also a core element of shamanistic cultures, that the shaman can 'become' the god of the tribe, or of an animal, etc.

References to this also appear in Hellenistic mystical literature, especially where it has assimilated ideas from older Egyptian mysticism. Here we find that Thoth or Hermes is somehow both a deity, who bestowed upon Egypt its amazing wisdom, and yet is also a human being – namely that human being to whom divine wisdom was imparted.

So, that huge and evocative image of the hanging figure on the rock outcrop here at the Externsteine probably represented the human vessel called Odhin, in his great struggle to obtain a special consciousness, this would enable him to become a vessel of the deity of the same name. Moreover, since the rocks could be subtly 'alive' to the holistic consciousness of earlier people, the carving of the figure of Odhin hanging on the Tree of Life on a towering rock outcrop would have had far more living ambience to the ancient Celts, than it has for us today. The runes were the central means through which the priesthood (i.e., the Weleda seeress, and others) could discover the will of deity – which was obviously a vital function for a guiding priesthood, if they are to keep their role in society.

The tree on which Odhin was hanging was no doubt Yggdrasil – the famous Tree of All-life symbolizing creation, mentioned often in the Edda. The Irmin column was a symbol of this. To be 'hanging on the tree' is therefore a metaphor for a priest merging his consciousness with cosmic realities; the 'tree' being the Tree of Life, the cosmos itself. This was a process that no doubt was carried out with difficulty, requiring tenacity, and causing stress.

So, to say that the man Odhin is consecrated unto himself, meant to the ancient priests that the man who is the vessel of the deity is being consecrated to that deity, and thus he will bear the name of that spiritual being. Such a person will also have to undergo severe ordeals to gain this higher consciousness. In any event, with these verses and the image of Odhin in the rock, it is very likely that we are looking at a noble theme; that of the initiatory journey of a leader of the old Nordic-Germanic peoples. Sceptics of course, view this apparent figure of a hanging entity, as accidental. And indeed the fissures in the rock are probably mainly accidental, but then enhanced by the priests. This figure of Odhin is of Celtic origin, carved long before the Christian era.

There is a curious similarity here to the Christian narrative of the Saviour who also voluntarily hangs on a wooden cross (if not exactly a tree). There is also the associated fact that, just as Odhin says he was wounded by the spear, so too the Christian Saviour was also pierced with a spear, by a Roman centurion, whilst hanging upon the wooden cross. But of course, it is not an exact parallel because, in the Christian event, the Saviour actually dies. With the Christian narrative there are parallels here too, as the intention of the Saviour is also to do with helping rescue humanity from some bleak cosmic future.

Later, when we come to our consideration of the unusual Christian relief carved on the main rock outcrop of the Externsteine, it will become clear that the artist has attempted to draw on this parallelism between the Edda and the Christian religion. Not that the message would have been kindly received, in the aftermath of the militant actions of Charlemagne. Let's now consider more of the abundant evidence that the

Externsteine was a sacred site in ancient times, long before the Teutons used it, or the church took it over.

The other strange figures in the rocks
Another intriguing feature to this site are the various recognizable forms, such as animals or faces, which seem to exist in the shape or outline of the rocks. For example, if you walk around behind the main rock, that is, Column One, you will see what appears to be the face of a man on the edge of the rocks, above the lake. And it appears that there is also a larger animal face, from inside of which this human face is emerging. When you visit, look at Column Five, you may see several images hidden there. To see some photos of these remarkable faces in the rocks, there are 2 German language websites that you can visit, which show one or more of these. You may see other faces or animals there, too.[13] Column Five has the face of a helmeted warrior, and at the very top, there appears to be a somewhat weathered outline of a dragon!

Now it is possible that these are just strange natural shapes, but it is much more likely that these shapes were deliberately made by people, long ago. Ancient peoples did make such shapes, often utilizing naturally occurring forms, and as the rocks deteriorated under the weather, later generations are left wondering whether a shape is their imagination or not. Such shapes are found in many countries, for example, on high in the Andes Mountains in Peru (the Marcahuasi plateau) is an extraodinary collection of carved hills, and in Queensland, Australia (the Glasshouse Mountains) there is also a number of similar hills. These hills seem to indicate that somehow this activity of carving shapes into rocks and hills may have been a form of sacred art, in remote times.

That there were people here in the Teutoburger Forest even some 7,000 years ago who used these rock outcrops for awareness of cosmic influences, became evident in 1982, when W. Matthes reported that on the higher parts of the Falcon Rock,

---

[13] 1: http://www.ur-europa.de/p25 and for a number of really intriguing photos see, 2: http://www.mystic-culture.de/kultplatz/externsteine/felsbilder

which is about 2 kilometres from the Externsteine columns, there were a number of seating places, roughly carved out from the rock. These were designed to facilitate observation of the heavens, towards the southwest. In recent times, another research project on the Falcon Stone, under Wolfhard Schlosser from Bochum University, confirmed the report from Matthes. It was carried out with official permission from the Park authorities. His party was helped by the Specialist Assistance Team of the German Alpine Association to scale this very steep rock, to investigate the site. (16)

They saw these seating places, and also noted that they were oriented to give a view of the sun rising on the winter solstice morning. Schlosser also reported that as the mountaineers were preparing the site to enable the others to ascend, they found signs of similar cutting-in of foot holes into the rock. But these had been done with rock tools, not iron tools, and hence may be dated back to the pre-historic (i.e., Neolithic) age. So, this area has been a sacred site, if only in a simple manner, for many thousands of years. It appears that this rock also has animal shapes carved into it, in particular a falcon (hence its name, the Falcon Rock), and also what appears to be a dragon. But when we see a shape that corresponds to a primary theme in the Edda, at the Externsteine, then it is reasonable to conclude that it has been specifically created under instructions from the Druidic priests.

Also, there is a large stone balanced precariously on the top of one of the rock towers. This is a quite specific feature of some sacred sites; it is called a 'wobble stone'; it can be seen clearly in illustrations 1 and 3. These are large stones that are very precariously balanced on top of another large stone, and are found especially at sites sacred to the Celts and the Megalithic peoples of Western Europe (we shall consider this 'wobble stone' feature later).

The deer of the sun
An example of such an animal form created in the rocks, is the figure seen on the back of Column Four, the column

with the boulder balancing precariously on top. There you can see a figure resembling a deer or similar animal, see illustration 4. In the Edda, in *The Sayings of Grimnir*, two grazing animals are described as belonging to the small number of creatures who have a special role in the great tree Yggdrasil, that is, the great multi-layered cosmos. One is a goat, Heidrun, and the other is a deer or 'hart' called Eikthyrnir, these two creatures exist on the upper section of Yggdrasil, which reaches up into the higher worlds. As *The Sayings of Grimnir* tell us, Eikthyrnir's antlers are viewed as a source of all life-giving waters here on the Earth,

> "The hart, in front of the Hall of the Father of Hosts (i.e. Wuotan), is called Eikthyrnir, it grazes on the foliage of Laerad. From its antlers, liquid drops down to Hwergelmir {i.e., the source of all rivers}. From these all streams arise."

So, the Edda seems to be saying that Eikthyrnir is a kind of cosmic archetype of all deer, and its name, which in Icelandic means 'woody thorns', highlights the special feature of the deer species. (17) Namely, its strange capacity to grow a plant-like growth on top of its head. This feature probably meant to the more holistic mindset of antiquity that the deer was a symbol of life-forces.[14] In the western world there is little in the way of concepts about subtle energies or life-forces, to help us to relate to the view of a deer as somehow special because of its antlers.

But the typical feature of Celtic art is the presence of many swirls, somewhat plant-like in their shapes. Perhaps these were meant to symbolize some kind of 'life-force', similar to the Eastern concept of Ch'i or 'prana'.[15] In any event, we can consider this carving on the rock is not Heidrun the goat, but rather Eikthyrnir, whose capacity of enhanced life-forces meant it was a symbol of the sun; the giver of life.

---

[14] This idea is presented especially in the works of Rudolf Steiner.

[15] The Goethe scholar Rudolf Steiner, who affirmed the concept of 'life-force', points out that the head and brain are the parts of the body that are the least 'living', and that this part of the body is the least endowed with life-force.

4 The Deer Eikthyrnir The rear side of the rock with the large boulder on top. The outline of a deer is clearly here, and probably, like the shape of Odhin (on the front side of this rock) was made by enhancing pre-existing fissures in the rocks.

This seems all the more likely, as Laerad is the name for the higher level of Yggdrasil, the great cosmic Tree of Life. (17) The deer is also used as **a symbol of the sun** in old Icelandic texts, and the sun's position on Yggdrasil naturally would be in the upper reaches of the great tree. So it is more likely to be the deer and not the goat which is carved here on the rock outcrop. We conclude that this outline of a deer has been intentionally made by Celtic priests, many centuries before the Christian era began. It is a symbol of the triumph of solar energies and their vivifying influence on life.

Chapter Five: spiritual-religious features of this site

The three day spiritual ritual: Hebrew, shamanistic, ancient Grecian

We noted how in earlier cultures there was an intense interest in attaining some form of interaction with higher realities and their gods. The priesthoods used a variety of techniques to achieve this, in particular a three-day sleep procedure. So what is this about a three day initiatory sleep? An important perspective here is that to the ancients, being asleep meant being out of the body, i.e., leaving the body. Thus the sleeper was, by default, in spiritual realms. So the ancient Greeks referred to sleep as the 'little brother of death', because in death one left the body in a permanent way, remaining in those spiritual realms, whereas in sleep one came back to the body each morning.

It is well known from anthropological studies that amongst cultures which have shamans as their spiritual guide, the process through which the acolyte becomes a shaman, also involves a three-day sleep. Many academic anthropological researchers have reported how a sleep which lasted for three days is required for the acolyte to become recognized as a shaman. For in this special period it is believed that the acolyte leaves their physical world and enters into the spirit world, to experience their deity or other spiritual realities. In such cultures this lethargic three-day process is often induced by ill-advised or harmful means, such as hallucinogenic drugs; but other, non-harmful methods may be employed. Graham Harvey in his 'Shamanism, a Reader' reports on this common feature, and many other accounts exist. (18) And as Leonid Lar reports,

> The encounter with death is a key moment of the shaman's initiation. Next the initiate receives a "new body" and is reborn to a new quality. During the initiation ritual a young shaman receives new supernatural qualities, which allow him to move fast in the space and time and allow for transformation from one state to another. According to the stories told by shamans

Yaptik and Mandakov they "were dead" for three days, did not eat or drink anything." (19)

In the Celtic world, as in ancient Egypt and in the Hellenistic Mystery centres, where this process was also undertaken wholesome techniques were used, although precise knowledge of the procedure in these cultures is kept confidential. In the Mystery Centres of such cultures, it seems that an acolyte would be placed in a stone sarcophagus as part of the initiation process (or placed upon a horizontal wooden cross, on the ground). From the few sparse notes about this process from antiquity, it is clear that an artificially induced sleep condition was designed to set the soul free from the body, so it could journey into spiritual realms, exactly as with the shamanistic cultures.

It was believed that during this time the acolyte would descend into the Underworld, and gain an objective view of his or her own lower qualities.. Then later in this process, the acolyte could ascend up to the deity of that religion, or even the divine beings from whom its own spirit derives. There is very little in the way of written explanation of this process, because all aspects of the old initiatory process were kept confidential. But this process is referred to in veiled language in Biblical texts and in Celtic literature of the British Isles.

In the Old Testament there is the story of Jonah, a Hebrew prophet, which also confirms the descent into the Netherworld or Hades. This is a famous story from the Bible, which tells of how a Hebrew mystic or so-called 'prophet' Jonah, was dumped overboard from a boat, and then swallowed by a whale. But three days later he was spat out onto the shore. This story is seen by people in the western mystical tradition as a disguised way of telling 'those in the know' about this very process. In this view, the sea then symbolizes the spirit world.

This theme of a descent into the Underworld (the realm of the Dead) is well known from the ancient Mysteries of the Hellenistic era. It is indicated in ancient Greek cults, and in mystical Hebrew texts. It was a specific part of Greek Mysteries, where it was known as the 'katabasis', which means the descent into the Netherworld. For example, at the oracle of Trophonius, situated at Lebadea, it was widely known that such descents into the Netherworld were the means by which the priests provided the wisdom that was being sought by their people. Quite a number of semi-mythical early heroes undertook this three day initiatory process.

Such heroes include Musaios and Eumolpos, and the famous Hercules, who were initiated at Eleusis. And reports circulated to the effect that the great sage Pythagoras went through this process, too. It is recounted in Homer's great saga, The Odyssey, how the famous hero Odysseus also descended into the Netherworld. However, in these myths and sagas it is described in a simplified and discreet way, because it was forbidden to mention the secrets of the initiatory process.

The three day spiritual ritual: Welsh
This mystical interpretation, which sees the three day immersion of Jonah in the ocean as a description of an initiatory process, is also found in texts from Celtic Britain, from old Wales, especially in the collection known as the Myvyrian Archaiology. In this material for example, is an account concerning the spiritual adventures of one Tuan Mac Cairell, in which there is an allusion to this initiatory three day sleep. A shamanistic character Tuan, tells how on one occasion he undergoes a sleep for three days and three nights and in this process, he became a fish living in the river: "Then I fasted for three days and three nights, when sleep fell upon me. And I passed into the shape of a river salmon, there and then." (20)

The interpretation of Jonah's three day journey inside a whale in the sea, as actually being a Hebrew version of the katabasis experience, is precisely how it was understood in mystical circles of old Celtic Britain. This is shown in a poem apparently written by King Urien Rheged, ruler of Cumbria in the 6th Century AD. King Urien was a prominent person in the mystical traditions of his times. He was the patron of the initiate bard Taliesin, who was probably in residence at his court. In one line of his poem, he asks the potent question, " **Who brought Jonah out of Kyd**?" (21) The term Kyd is actually short for Kyridwen or Keridwen; and this is the Celtic name for the realm of the dead and its spirits, and also for the goddess ruling this realm.

These cryptic statements indicate the existence of a firm belief in, and therefore probably the actual use of, the three-day initiation sleep in the old Celtic world. For it is clear that Urien Rheged understood the story of Jonah to be about the initiatory process, which involves a descent into the Underworld, in some kind of soul journey.

The so-called arcosolium, a ritual sarcophagus?
The next feature to observe here is the initiatory sarcophagus, it is undamaged, and exposed to the sky, see illustration 5. But the presence of the special kind of sarcophagus at a site that is not actually a burial site is a feature that is still left out of archaeological discussion. But since there was evidence of church activity in this site, it was natural to define all its features as medieval, including this sarcophagus. Thus Kroesen for example writes,

> There is a curious example of a Chapel of the Holy Sepulchre in Germany in the steep rocks of the Externsteine. In 1093 this site was annexed by the Benedictine monastery of Abingdof in Paderborn. At the behest of Bishop Heinrich von Werl, an imitation of the Holy Places in Jerusalem was cut in the rocks.
>
> (22)

This is simply conjecture; it is not known that this bishop commissioned such a structure. One notes that this writer does say that the sarcophagus here is a *curious example*. And in a foot-note the author says that these rock towers "served as a sacrificial site in a pre-Christian cult, which was later Christianized". There is no proof of the bishop ever ordering

5   Top : Externsteine sarcophagus, not a church replica but an initiatory feature

Bottom: Similar sarcophagus in a remote sacred Bulgarian site, 1900 BC

such work to be done here, although he may well have caused a baptismal font to be carved out of the floor in one chamber, and possibly had a small recluse cell hollowed out, up on one wall, for religious contemplation. In fact it is only an assumption that the bishop of Paderborn, Heinrich von Werl actually had the sarcophagus carved, or the chambers hollowed out. The religious documents that establish the involvement of the medieval church at the Externsteine do not at all prove that the Church actually created this site.

The idea that the sarcophagus also was created for an ancient spiritual ritual, has not yet found acceptance amongst mainstream historians. This is understandable since modern society has difficulty understanding the people of ancient times, especially their quest to become aligned to spirit beings and cosmic influences. But anthropological research into shamanistic cultures has established how significant such a rite was to these people. Such a sarcophagus was used in ancient sacred sites for the three-day temple sleep, which was part of what we today would call an initiatory process, similar to those used in shamanistic cultures.

As we noted earlier, there is a parallel to the sarcophagus here; it exists in southern Bulgaria, where an unusual kind of tomb has been uncovered, perched up on a hill. It is dated to about 1900 BC, and is similar in appearance to the sarcophagus at the Externsteine, see illustration 5. It has a mysterious quality, because archaeologists are aware that a construction of this kind in such a position would never be a real tomb. It is located in an important religious site of the ancient Thracians or Bulgarians; so it need not be a tomb at all, but a religious monument. People refer to it as the tomb of Orpheus, a semi-god from ancient Grecian mythology. It was very probably designed for similar spiritual rituals as the one at the Externsteine, and will be of approximately the same age.

These rituals formed a central part of religious activity in many shamanistic cultures, and also in the Hellenistic Mysteries (more about that later). As archaeological research progresses, more such sites will probably found. The conservative view is that the sarcophagus at the Externsteine was constructed by a Christian bishop, who wished to have a replica of the 'arcosolium' or tomb of Jesus, as represented in the Church of the Holy Sepulchre at Jerusalem. And indeed about 50 of these replicas have been found throughout Germany.

An arcosolium is an arched recess which is used as a tomb, it has a low wall built up in the front, and once the body was placed in the space between this wall and the back wall, a vertical slab was placed over it. Later versions of an 'arcosolium', after ca. 150 AD, would have the arched recess cut down to waist height, and then a cavity would be cut out for the floor, to receive the body. Then a vertical front wall placed over the tomb. Here at the Externsteine this space was never enclosed. But is the stone sarcophagus here a medieval arcosolium, representing the Church of the Holy Sepulchre at Jerusalem? No, it is not.

For, of the 50 replicas of the Church of the Holy Sepulchre that were built in early Germany, not one of them has a sarcophagus in it. Instead, Jesus is usually depicted as lying on the floor surface of the arched recess. So it cannot be called a replica of this church, since it deviates from the pattern. But there is more to say here. Around this sarcophagus there are steps that lead up to a small flat rock platform. And from this platform, on the spring and autumn equinox, the sun can be seen rising up directly above the wobble-stone. This stone was an important ritual object; it is perched on top of a rock tower. We shall explore its meaning later. There are never any such astronomical observation platforms in a medieval monastic site.

But furthermore, excavations in the 1930's have shown that sections of the stone wall around the sarcophagus extend down about 1.5 metres below current ground level. So, at some remote time in the past, before the soil accumulated over several millennia, the sarcophagus would have been at head height for any one passing nearby. (23) So it is not a burial coffin; it is very likely an initiatory sarcophagus. That is, a rock cavity which is designed to allow some form of mystical experience to be carried out. A customary Christian or non-Christian burial coffin would not have such features.

Such sarcophagi in exposed and remote situations are to be found in places where long ago the Celts had established their sacred sites. Such sarcophagi or hollowed-out cavities in rocks like this one have been found in the Alsace region, which is a special part of central Europe, with a long history of Celtic spirituality. Near the town of St. Jean les Saverne, on Michaelsberg, is the Chapel of St. Michel (or St. Michael); it is about 448 yards (410m) high up on the top of a hill that rises spectacularly straight up above the fields below. Just a little below this chapel, as Gesänger points out, one finds a cave that has a sarcophagus carved out of the wall, near its entrance. Since such a sarcophagus-like shape hollowed out in such a setting is not intended as a burial site, it is also very likely to be an initiatory sarcophagus.

Quite a number of human-shaped sarcophagi have been carved out on the top of the rock outcrop at the beautiful and evocative hill of Odilienberg in the Alsace region. These sarcophagi have been placed along the very edge of this steep mountain. Their purpose is not known for certain, but they appear to be a cultic feature. It is quite common for a spiritual site to become used for burials long after their original purpose has been forgotten. So it is possible that some of these sarcophagi were later used as coffins, and certainly there were also some coffins of this same shape at Odilienberg, but these are found several metres underground in the centre of the site, near the old chapels.

So, the sarcophagus at the Externsteine is an ancient Celtic feature, used for spiritual purpose, and has a similar appearance and purpose as the one found in Bulgaria. It is in fact likely that it was in the sarcophagus at this site, that the acolyte who was to become the greatly revered vessel of Odhin, underwent his spiritual experience, referred to in the Edda as 'hanging on the cosmic tree'. This would have made the site even more sacred to the Celtic and to the later Teutonic tribes-people.

St. Peter or the one eyed Odhin?
The next feature to observe is that of 'St. Peter'. This figure is carved on Column One, but a closer examination of it leads one to doubt that it is St. Peter who is depicted here. One reason is that this figure bears no relationship to the Christian carving of the Deposition from the Cross. It is quite removed from this relief, separated by an entrance to a small grotto (now covered by a metal grill). Indeed it stands as a kind of sentry or guardian, facing the threshold of an opening into a grotto. The opening that has cut into the rock takes one into this grotto, and from there, one can go into the main large grotto.

The figure has been damaged, so its features are not easy to see. The head is fully formed, and it is separated from the rock wall, whilst the rest of the figure is only slightly differentiated from its rock setting. The head area has been damaged, and this presents a major problem in identifying whom it represents. It appears to the visitor today as a one eyed figure; but its second eye may have been destroyed in the past, as were its mouth and nose. **Or, it may have never been given a second eye.** It is very significant that the damage sustained has made it difficult to know whether it was a one eyed figure, or a two eyed figure, as this is vital factor in determining whom this figure represents.

The first option is that it depicts St. Peter; if this is so, then his face, especially his eye on the left, has been damaged. The other option is that it represents Odhin, the one eyed god, in which case, **he never had a second eye**. Because, according to the Edda, Odhin has only one eye. Now, one could easily conclude that the figure is holding what appears to be a key, and it is generally said that St. Peter 'carries the key of heaven'. However, a careful look at the figure shows that some of his hair is tied tightly around to one side. This kind of hairstyle is precisely the hairstyle of Celtic men, whereas it was never the hairstyle of a Hebrew person. (24) This figure is standing like a guardian of the entrance to the grotto, it is not placed in any direct link to the Christian relief.

Now, the second option is that it is a Celtic figure, as indeed the hairstyle indicates, and if he is one eyed, then this is nothing less than a carving of Odhin! He will be holding a staff, not a key. So the present key shape would be the result of his staff being altered by Christian monks, under the direction of Charlemagne. Summing up, if this were a carving of St. Peter, then the left eye has been obliterated through the damage done to the statue, and the key shaped rod is original.

So which is it, St. Peter or Odhin? See illustration 6 for attempts to reconstruct the original form. In addition to the Celtic hairstyle, there are several features in favour of it being an ancient, non-Christian carving. There is the fact that the statue is much more weathered than the Christian relief, giving it an indistinct appearance; it is therefore much older. Further, Speckner and Stamm point out that the prominent right eye(socket) shows signs of having been subject to fire, which indicates another way in which the carving was harmed. (23)

Also the figure is carrying not only a staff (or key) but also a second object, yet a second object is never shown with depictions of St. Peter. But, because of the weathering, and also quite possibly, the defacing by Charlemagne in earlier centuries, this second object is not clearly visible, but it may well be a sword within its scabbard. In the Celtic-Germanic people a scabbard ended in a roughly rectangular shape, not in a pointed shape. But we wish to present another, more likely possibility. This second object depicts a board on which once long ago, the magic runes were carved, but the runes have been obliterated. Odhin obtained the runes through his spiritual experience and may well have been depicted originally here as carrying them.

70

LEFT A very old carving. Photo has been retouched to improve visibility, Rune signs are added.

RIGHT
Siegfried Schröder's reconstruction. Hair style is typical of Teutonic men.
A hairline and nose added for clarity.

6 Photos of the figure of Odhin as Guardian to the entry to the grotto This figure is incorrectly called the St. Peter figure.

Now the fact that the head has been damaged is an important clue in identifying this figure. As we noted above, the left side of the face has been very severely damaged, so it is hard to say whether it ever had a second eye, namely a left eye. So, it is **exactly this damage that actually makes it hard to confirm** those features that make Wuotan different from St. Peter. A suspicious circumstance! A major reason that this carving is likely to be a Celtic work of art is that a very important feature of Odhin was in fact that **he was described as one eyed in the Edda**.

Furthermore, this damage to the carving strongly indicates that it was an ancient pre-Christian artwork. For if damage ever occurred to any artwork at the Externsteine, it was perpetrated by Charlemagne's forces against the original 'pagan' artwork – because the Teutonic tribes people would not harm their own sacred site. And it is most unlikely to have been perpetrated by the conquered Germanic warriors against the now triumphant Christians. But the reverse is very likely – the triumphant Christian power attacking the heritage of the conquered people. The Roman Christian authorities had a standard practice of either destroying a monument, or altering these older 'pagan' carvings, in order to claim them as Christian.

So, the damage says in effect, "Let no-one find out that this was once, long ago, a one eyed figure, namely Odhin; let us now make it appear a reasonable likeness of St. Peter." Hence the runes were obliterated from the rune board, and the staff was changed into a key shape. This is all the more reasonable as a conclusion, because the damage to the left side of the head had to be deliberately and very specifically carried out, because that side of the head **is actually hard up against the wall**, and hence somewhat inaccessible. The attack on the Externsteine by Charlemagne occurred in 772 AD, and it is obvious that the extensive Christian relief was carved onto the rock column some decades later, when it was safe to proceed.

That is, only when there was no real risk of it being defaced by an uprising of Germanic people. This also means that the

Christian relief was carved here after 804 AD, which is the year when the leader of the Germanic uprising, Wittekind, agreed to be baptized, and cease his campaign against Charlemagne. So our conclusion here is that this figure is an ancient Celtic feature, depicting Odhin, and that it was harmed, i.e., altered, in the arson and destruction by Charlemagne of 772 AD.

But before we look at the one-eyed aspect of Odhin, to confirm our conclusion that it is a pre-Christian carving, let's just note that it cannot be St. Peter, because he is never depicted carrying a staff as well as a long sword in a scabbard, (or a long rectangular cloth, or rectangular board). In Christian art, there are set rules as to how a person is depicted, known as 'iconography'. St. Peter is always shown as having a short beard, with a full set of thick curly hair, although after ca. 500 AD, his hair might be balding from the back of the head (but not the front). [16]

St. Peter certainly never has a Celtic warrior's long hairstyle, tied back to one side. Such rules as these were strictly followed, to allow the populace throughout Christendom to recognize the particular saint depicted on any work of art. Also, but often overlooked, is the fact that St. Peter was never depicted carrying a key, **but it was always a pair of keys**, because Christ's words are, "I will give to you **the keys** to the kingdom of heaven". Peter usually carries his two keys, and he could also have a Bible (or a short scroll), or a shepherd's staff. But he doesn't carry a staff as well as some second long, substantial object.

So, in terms of artistic depiction, the figure on the wall here is scarcely able to represent St. Peter, but it is well able to represent Odhin, with his one eye, his sidewards hair style, a staff and his rune board (or sword). The Edda tells us that Odhin had to sacrifice one eye, in order to drink from a fountain controlled by a mysterious figure called Mimir. Mimir is described as the wisest of the gods, and Odhin, to gain wisdom, has to place one eye in this fountain, before he can drink from it.

---

[16] See website; www.catholic.org/encyclopedia and www.aug.edu/augusta/iconography

So this is another ordeal that the 'avatar' priest had to undergo. A text in the Edda, called the Seeress's Prophecy (Song of the Voluspa) tells us about this briefly "...I know of Odhin's eye hidden in Mimir's fountain..." It was only by sacrificing his eye that he could gain the wisdom of the runes. This carving, whose features are now somewhat obscured, is an illustration of a core theme of the Celtic religion, as preserved in the Edda; it goes back to a time some centuries before Christianity, to the Celtic people who established their sacred place here at the Externsteine.

Several further indications show that this one eyed figure is of Celtic origin. Firstly, Odhin with his rune board is in effect guarding the entrance to the grotto. This is a strong indicator of a mystical purpose, because this means that Odhin is a kind of guardian of the threshold across into a sacred space. The next point is that this space, only a small bare room, has two very significant features. The ceiling is domed, that is, it has a cupola shaped ceiling, and yet there is actually no sign of any chisel blows, cutting away the rock, to create such a concave feature! This is really intriguing, as rock carvings chiselled out from hard stone in earlier ages always show, upon close examination, definite chisel imprints.

The next unusual feature is that a very carefully carved shaft has been cut through the wall, to the right of the entrance. This rectangular opening has a deliberate, obscuring bend on one side of its wall. You can faintly see the opening of this rectangular shaft in illustration 9. It is just underneath a curve in the long tail of the dragon. This bend in one wall of the shaft means that it deliberately reduces drastically the amount of light that can enter the grotto. The next feature of this grotto, based on all this, is that sunlight only enters this grotto on the morning of the summer solstice. For a few minutes, the floor of this space is lit up by the sunlight of the summer solstice, indicating that it was used for spiritual purposes associated with the summer sun. (23)

Now as the evidence for a pre-Christian origin of the site continues to mount, the conclusion is strengthened that the Externsteine was not established by the Teutonic tribes as a sacred site, but by another, earlier Celtic group of people. The period of Celtic activity here probably began about 3,000 BC. It is quite possible that the priests of the indigenous European people established their sacred site here, millennia before the Celts appeared. But the Externsteine probably had several phases of development under the Celts – in any event, this certainly was long before the Roman-Germanic wars, which is the time when Teutonic tribes first begin to be historically identifiable as specific tribes, and who could be thought of as the ancestors of modern Germans.

At least a part of these Teutonic tribes originated from the Nordic world of Scandinavian peoples, who shared in the religion of the Druids. So there would be no difficulty for the Teutonic people to assimilate the earlier religious practices that had been centred at the Externsteine by the Celtic Druids. So this feature, the one-eyed god, like the large outline of Odhin hanging on the Tree of Life, had its origin at least 4,500 years ago, and possibly long before that – it is hard to date the layer of cultural-religious history to which it belongs.

It shows us that the Externsteine was a place where the primary themes of the religion belonging to the Germanic-Celtic people, and their predecessors, were depicted. The one-eyed Odhin represents another aspect to this god, and one that also requires sacrifice. However it is worth noting, in order to appreciate this wonderful site in the Teutoburger Forest that neither the nine days hanging of Odhin, nor his sacrifice of an eye, are to be taken literally. And the actual instituting of such actions in sinister 'religious' rituals only occurs when the religion became devitalized and decadent, or the tool of less civilised, more militant peoples.

The theme of the sacrifice of an eye, or the theme of a significant person who has only one eye, is very likely a reference to a spiritual theme, for it occurs in mystical literature. For example, there is the story of the one, additional eye of Buddha, referred to as the 'third eye'. This is understood to depict an organ of higher perception. It is the 'third eye', and is understood to be a kind of cognizing organ for spirit realms, which exists in the person's soul. There is also the episode in Homer's Odyssey, which is a story of the spiritual quest, where Odysseus confronts a one eyed giant. When Odysseus attacks him, the giant loses his one eye. This same theme is found in the fairy tales of the central and northern European peoples, and they are the descendants of the Celtic-Teutonic people.

For example, in the late medieval German fairy stories of the brothers Grimm, is the story of "One eye, Two eyes and Three eyes". And in a fairy Tale from Norway, this theme occurs in the story of "Lillekort's Adventures", where the hero has to remove three times the one eye from a malignant one-eyed hag, in order to gain wisdom or special powers. (25) But the myth cannot be saying that the human vessel of Odhin actually had to lose one of his physical eyes. This makes no sense at all in terms of attaining wisdom. There is another possibility; did the myth-makers think that he had to 'sacrifice', or close down, this solitary 'eye' up on the forehead, at least for a while? Of course this idea then invokes the question, why close down the very organ that in the view of ancient cultures, gives the priest access to the spirit realms? The Edda doesn't really clarify this riddle, but the simplistic image of a one-eyed Odhin is a richly evocative figure in these texts.[17]

It is intriguing to note that centuries later, the European and British became the first people to turn away from the religious consciousness of the medieval and pre-medieval world, and to pioneer the era of modern industrialization and humanism. Did the Druids foresee a future age of scientific rationalism, to be pioneered by the western world? Was this part of the prophesied Dark Age of 'Ragnarok' or the Twilight of the Gods mentioned in the Song of the Seeress? It is simply fascinating to walk around the Externsteine site and consider such questions as these.

---

[17] This idea is put forward by the Goethe scholar Rudolf Steiner

Priestly Sacellum or astronomical observatory ?
Now we come to a consideration of the so-called sacellum, a remarkable chamber perched high up on top of Column Two. Here we find features that would never be incorporated into a sacred site built by the Christian church. This chamber is heavily damaged; its roof and two sides are missing. So it has been open to the weather for centuries. This is itself a sign of a 'pagan' origin, because it was this pagan origin which caused the wrath of the church, that is, its emperor Charlemagne. It was a dark enclosed room, prior to the damage wrought by Charlemagne in 772, during the 2 to 3 days that he camped there with his troops.

It faces the northeast, the point where the sun rises on the summer solstice; see illustration 7. And in this north-eastern wall a round hole has been very carefully carved. On the summer solstice (June 21st) the rising sun sends a beam of light through this hole, into the chamber. So in terms of the seasonal cycle, it has a practical importance, in that the priests could determine key dates of the seasonal year. But there is much more to this feature in the wall. For the wall is quite thick, and the hole has been carved or ground in such a way as to form a conical shape, the sloping wall has an angle of $4.2°$. So a conical rod – like an ice-cream cone – could be put into the hole. If this were done, then to what would the sharp end of a cone point?

Research into this was done in the 1990's by a German scientist, Wolfhard Schlosser, working in the new field of astro-archaeology, and his work has revealed key facts about this precisely designed aperture. (23) He found that a conical rod placed in the hole would point exactly to the most northern point in the heavens reached by the Moon, in what is called its 'major standstill'. This refers to the 18.6 year cycle of the Moon's journey along its pathway around the Earth. It is also known as the lunar node cycle.

At this time, every 18.6 years, its energies are at their most potent in the weather and plant life, causing very high tides, more humid atmospheric conditions, etc. It is interesting to note here that Stonehenge is also specifically designed to enable observation of this approximately 19 year cycle. These discoveries by Schlosser are acknowledged by other scientists working in astronomy and in physics. One of these was Professor Clemens Woda, the leader of the scientific team who investigated those burn marks, we mentioned earlier, using thermal-luminescence dating technology. (3)

So, this chamber allowed an observer to track the nodal cycle of the moon. A node is the point of intersection of the pathway of the Moon and the pathway of the Sun. This monitoring of the moon's nodal cycle allows a person to predict the next lunar or solar eclipse, because eclipses occur on the new Moon or the full Moon, nearest to the time when the Sun in its journey, passes by the node. But this feature allowed the priests/priestesses to do more than just predict solar and lunar eclipses, as a purely physical fact. Celestial phenomena were seen as an expression of spiritual realities in the Celtic and Teutonic world, and indeed elsewhere, too.

For example, the old Nordic myths describe eclipses as being caused when an evil wolf temporarily swallows the Sun or Moon; this implies that eclipses are a time when unwholesome energies abound. In any event, it is very likely that one of the activities at the Externsteine involved providing rituals designed to give spiritual protection for the people from the malignant energies released at an eclipse. It is interesting to note that at Stonehenge, observation of the lunar nodes is also a really major feature, just as important as the observation of the sun rising at the summer solstice.

In passing, we note there is also a small stone altar in this damaged chamber, below the conical shaped aperture. It is very likely that a sacred object was placed on this for ritual purposes, including no doubt on the day of the summer solstice. A

7 The now roofless upper chamber; facing mid-summer sunrise. The arrow indicates the ugly face (lower self).

medieval report exists about the activities of the church in the Paderborn area, which mentions 'an upper altar' at a site in the Teutoburger Forest; this has to be referring to the Externsteine. So it is not surprising that people have speculated that this altar was used for celebrating Mass, and shows the Christian origins of the site one. But reports of such activity by the monks are simply evidence of the efforts by the church to Christianize the site. It is not proof that the chamber was constructed by the monks.

The Irmin Column or Celtic Tree of Life

We saw earlier that Charlemagne spent 2 to 3 days at 'the place of the Irmin Column', which he set on fire. And we have been able to conclude that it is very likely that the site which he destroyed was indeed the Externsteine – the only site of sufficient sacredness and importance to become the focus of the destructive campaign by Charlemagne, to undermine the unifying religious loyalties of the tribes-people. So it was at the Externsteine where, in addition to the fascinating chambers and carvings, the greatest Irmin column was set up. What was this column? It was a substantial wooden column, the primary sacred symbol of the Saxons. Scholars have to deduce what the column actually represents, as nothing is written about it by the Saxons. But the consensus is that the Irmin column represents Creation, the cosmic tree of life, and also its Creator.

The Irmin column is a simplified depiction of this cosmic tree, known as Yggdrasil, which encompasses the nine realms of the cosmos, and the hosts of divine spiritual beings, and evil beings, and intermediate beings all of whom dwell in these realms. It appears that its name also refers to the Creator of all these realms, although it is difficult for the scholars to determine the name of this deity. It may have been another version of Odhin's name, or possibly Tyr, another of the Nordic gods.

It is said that there is no formal pictorial representation of this column, but as we shall discover, it is in fact depicted right at the Externsteine site, inside the strange Christian relief that was imposed

80

on the site. Furthermore, it is to be found in some old German churches in the nearby area. There is only one written description of the Irmin Column, and that comes from a contemporary of Charlemagne, a monk from the Fulda monastery, Rudolf von Fulda (died 865). He would have either seen the column before it was destroyed, or witnessed its destruction. He writes:

> The Saxons worshipped an upright tree trunk, erected in the open air, of considerable dimensions, which they called 'Irmin column' in their mother tongue; which means in Latin 'columna universalis', that is a column which supports the All.   (26)

So the Irmin column is a kind of Tree of Life, or depiction of the cosmos; and each tribal nation, or larger groups within a tribe, would have set up such a column at their meeting place. It is very obvious that a huge version of this venerated column would have been once standing at the Externsteine. Now, we see again why the official Frankish documents do not state clearly, but only make a vague, indirect reference to the fact that Charlemagne had committed such offences against the Saxon religion. It would have been particularly unwise for his official chroniclers to boast about such an action, especially in view of the fury that it caused. As we noted earlier, the official records state: "He (Charlemagne) conquered the {place called} Eresburg and {then} reached the place which is called the Irmin column, and he set this place on fire."

An effort is made here to let it be subtly known, without spelling it out, that the Emperor moved on from Eresburg, deeper into the Teutoburger Forest, to the great Irmin column at the Externsteine, and undertook his destructive and actually deeply unchristian actions; actions which backfired badly on him. The Irmin column, which was destroyed, was later depicted as part of the Christian relief, but it is shown as bent over. But one can see what it would have been – a tall column that has two curved parts on the top, sweeping off the left and the right, with some scrollwork on them. To see what the Irmin Column looked like on the Externsteine Christian relief, and a view of it, unbent, see illustration 8.

This is no doubt an accurate depiction of the Irmin column, which has otherwise never been depicted by the Saxons. However, it is not the only depiction of it, for such was the impact of the actions of Charlemagne that other church leaders decided to make a copy of the Irmin column, shown in some sort of submissive position, in their churches. One such place is in the Abdinghof monastery, located in central Paderborn, not far from the Externsteine. This building was established in 1015 AD, and incorporates an Irmin column on the top of one of the pillars.

Another depiction of the Irmin column, dating from only 50 years after the attack on the Externsteine, is to be found in the Church of St. Michael in the town of Fulda, in the state of Hesse. Here the monks built a small column, like a tree trunk, in the middle of the crypt, as if supporting the ceiling.

And, according to various scholars of church history, in the cathedral at Hildesheim there is a tall column depicting the Virgin Mary, but which has been referred to by the locals for many centuries, as 'the Irmin column'. The column is regarded as deriving from Roman times, and the area around Hildesheim was once populated with many Germanic-Celtic settlements. (27).

This is mute testimony to the take over by the victors of the religion belonging to a defeated culture. Careful textual and historical analysis has allowed us to conclude that indeed the Externsteine was the great central site of the Teutonic people and that a major Irmin column was once there.

But in addition, there is some help from archaeology in this regard, for in front of Column Two, excavations revealed

83

8 B Artist's reconstruction of the upright Irmin Column, as it may have looked in its undamaged state.

8 A The Irmin Column, bent over, carved on the Externsteine as a footstool: detail from the Christian relief

that there was once a pit about 9 ft (2.7m) in depth. This pit has been filled in long ago and lies underneath a layer of topsoil. In the pit is a mixture of sand and clay, mixed with fragments of coal. It is quite possible that this is where the great Irmin column, of perhaps 5 to 8 metres height, had once stood, before it was cut down and burnt in 772 AD.

Finally, we can note that there is also a feature here that is in effect, a kind of speaker's podium carved from rock and with steps leading up to it. It is in front of Column One, which has the main grotto and carvings, so it is some distance to the right of the great Irmin Column. This feature is very hard to date, but is very probably of Teutonic origin; a place from where the Weleda could address the assembled people.

Chapter Six: The meaning of its Artworks

The Christian relief: key to the site's medieval history

Let's now look at the Christian carving on the main column. Although it is not part of the Celtic-Germanic features of this site, it is a striking feature which helps us to discover some of the hidden history of Externsteine. The carving is large, measuring 5.47 yards x 3.94 yards (5 m x 3.6m). We see firstly that it depicts the taking down of Jesus from the cross, and that it is placed very centrally on Column One, (above a severely weathered carving), see illustration 9.

As one would expect, over the centuries in Christendom, quite a number of artists have depicted the event of the taking down of the body of Christ from the cross, for the church. But no one has depicted it in the remarkable way that the unknown artist has done at the Externsteine! On the left is Mary (her head is missing), and on the right is St. John, holding a book; so far, this is quite traditional. In the centre is the body of Jesus, which is lying on the shoulders of a man, who is taking him down (one of his arms is missing), this man is understood to be Joseph of Arimathea.

But a little higher up another man is to be seen, with one arm around the central part of the cross. He has just helped to release Jesus from it. This man is understood to be Nicodemus, a believer in Christ, who was also a member of the Sanhedrin or central council of the Judean priesthood. In the Gospel of St. John, Nicodemus is described as helping Joseph of Arimathea to bury Jesus. So, this inclusion of Nicodemus shows an inspiration from this Gospel, as the other three Gospels do not mention him in regard to this matter.

Nicodemus is further associated with Joseph of Arimathea in very old Christian texts which are not in the Bible, these are partly historical, partly legendary texts. Further, as we noted earlier, Nicodemus is in effect standing upon a bent-over column (although his legs are missing); just what this column actually

9 The Deposition of Christ Carolingian carving on the Externsteine about AD 804

represents has been a controversial theme. We have seen that Charlemagne attacked the site, and the Frankish records are discreet about this, because Charlemagne's actions here were politically disastrous, and any boasting about this cultural crime by the conqueror would have exacerbated the violent anger it caused.

In no other Christian artwork does a person stand upon a bent-over symbolic 'pagan' column in the process of removing the body of Jesus from the cross. It is quite clear that Nicodemus is standing upon the Irmin Column, and it is equally clear that there is a message here. The sacred symbol of the Christian religion, namely the cross, stands tall and strong, dominating above the now bent-over (i.e., defeated) Irmin Column. We see here the stern unyielding demands of Charlemagne to his artists. But in fact there are indications in this carving that the more insightful and spiritual Christians disapproved of the actions of their overlord, see illustration 10.

The foremost Christian authority at Charlemagne's court was a benevolent Christian priest, Alcuin, whose objections to Charlemagne's use of very un-Christian violence is on record. It appears to be Alcuin's conviction that the Christian message of a God who actually dynamically loves each human being is deeply true, and a truth entirely incompatible with the aggressive behaviour of Charlemagne.

Alcuin would also have known that in Britain, the early 'Culdee' Christian priests, whose church soon ceased to exist after the arrival of Roman Christianity, met the Druids on equal terms and conversed respectfully with them. But Charlemagne decided upon a campaign of military domination, and as a result, the most important ancient sacred site in northern Europe was extensively damaged.

And a dialogue between the representatives of an ancient mystical nature religion and the intruding Roman version of the Christian faith was made impossible. But perhaps that was only a remote chance in this particular cultural context.

One can see in some of the features of this carving the wish of benevolent Christians to try to communicate in a kindly fashion with the Saxons. For example, above the bent-over Irmin Column, Jesus is not a stern judge, judging the pagans, and inaugurating the terrible Judgment of the World. Rather he personally has just been subjected to a terrible ordeal, and has died. But, on the other hand, to communicate the message of real power behind this new religion, the Saxons are also given here, with tactfulness, a sign of an inherent power and triumph to the Christian religion: the figure of God high above.

For the message of the church is of course, that God's power will ensure that Jesus shall triumph over this death, and be resurrected. Already this tells us that the relief was carved some decades after the attack of 772 AD; at a time when the fury of the Saxons had abated, and their power was weakened enough to make such a religious-political statement culturally possible.

In fact, it would not have started before 804 AD, the year when the leader of the resistance, Wittekind, was won over, converting to Christianity. In addition, as a sign of the church adopting in a positive tone, features of the Saxon's nature spirituality, the Sun and the Moon are depicted there as witnesses. They each are shown with a face, representing the spirits who are the souls of these celestial bodies. And both these beings appear to be weeping, holding a cloth to their face.

Such depictions as these embrace the Celtic view of Nature as being en-souled with many spirit beings. To the Saxons these celestial bodies were an outer expression of an inner living host of spiritual beings, and here they are, sadly witnessing the Crucifixion. Many art historians, no doubt mislead by the misinformation campaign from the court of Charlemagne concerning the Externsteine, have dated this relief to early in the 12th century, concluding that it is a Romanesque artwork!

But, this is not an accurate interpretation, for as we examine the carving further it is quite clearly seen to be a Carolingian artwork. That is, it dates to the late 8th or early 9th century AD.

To proceed in our exploration of this relief, we should just note that Art in this period of European history may show the older, rigid Byzantium artistic influence. It may also attain a degree of Naturalism, which means the artist succeeds in realistically portraying the people or animals and plants in his artwork. However, artworks of this era can also show some degree of expressiveness; which means bringing some emotive content into the depicting of a theme.

Now, it is a feature of Carolingian art that **it retains both these types of art inside the one work of art** – the naturalism and expressiveness. But in addition, Carolingian art mixed these two qualities together with the rigid, abstractly lineal qualities of the Byzantium period, too. A careful look at this large relief carving shows that all these qualities are within this powerful masterpiece at the Externsteine; these are not qualities belonging to the later Gothic art.

Furthermore, it is well known that Charlemagne embraced the use of art to help in the political and cultural re-organizing of life in the conquered peoples, as he set about his work of enlarging and consolidating his Christian empire. This remarkable relief would have been carved 35 years or so after the damage was inflicted on the Externsteine. A time when contact between the Christians and the Saxons was possible again; perhaps about 805-810 AD, and thus in the final years of Alcuin's life.

Another dating indicator here is given in the clothing of the people. St. Mary and St. John both have traditional Palestinian clothing, as represented in Byzantium and other very early Christian artwork. But the two men, Joseph and Nicodemus, who are in fact instrumental in helping Jesus, in releasing his body, are actually dressed in Saxon tunics, complete with Saxon hats! These tunics are not the long type worn by men in the 12th century; they are the shorter type, **of the type worn in the 8th century**. And both men have hats, but these are not Near Eastern hats. As Gesänger points out, Joseph also seems to have a Germanic metal helmet, whilst Nicodemus is wearing a woven straw helmet, and under that, he has a cap made of either leather or cloth. These are 8th or 9th century headgear for Saxon men. (28) In Christian art from this era, these two would normally be either bare-headed or wear a hat typical of Palestine of 2,000 years ago.

So, another message appears here – 'You Saxons are welcome to be part of the great drama of the Messiah's mission, and also you are indeed included amongst the people whom he is saving.' This would be an especially relevant message for the Saxons some years after the destruction of the Externsteine had elapsed, from a church hoping to establish its message. But by the 12th century, it would not any longer be necessary to depict the conquered and bent Irmin Column, for the Saxons had long ago disappeared; but nor would it be necessary to so graphically include the still hostile Saxons in a reconciliatory way. For by the 12th century the fierce opposition of the Saxons to the Christendom was in the past; the Holy Roman Empire had conquered.

Another point about the dating of this relief is perhaps relevant here, that the cross, which was in effect a crucifix, is a very prominent feature, Now, it is surprising to learn that the crucifix was not among the original symbols of Christianity. It had been formally instituted as the symbol of Christianity only in 680 AD – it was not the formal official symbol until then! Indeed for the first four hundred years after the death of Jesus, it was never used. So this carving was using a symbol only recently established, and of which there were probably very few in northern Germany at the time. So this depiction here of a kind of crucifix was probably first time that it was depicted in this part of central Europe.

However there are two further, more potent dating indicators, the prominent flag that the upper figure is holding, and the scene depicted below. This figure above represents God (called the Father-God in German), and he is holding three things. One is a small person, another is the prominent flag on a rod, and thirdly there is an unusual cross. Now the flag is very flat and at its end is divided into three tongues, thus forming what is called an

Oriflamme. This object is a well-known flag from medieval times, when French kings used it as a Standard or flag at military campaigns or processions. This is why the sculptor has made it very flat, to represent a thin piece of cloth.

What is significant here is that Frankish historical traditions tell us that during the ceremony on Christmas Day in 800 AD in Rome, when Pope Leo III crowned Charlemagne Emperor, this standard was bestowed upon him as sign of papal blessing. This was the birth of the Holy Roman Empire. The Oriflamme had been in use since early in the 8th century, and now it had become a specially decorated official standard for the Emperor. So, the message for the Saxons in the carving here is; Charlemagne's power and authority comes from God, and if the great column which represents your pagan God has now gone, you now see that the true God has empowered the emperor. The Externsteine relief testifies to the recent momentous event, the birth of the Holy Roman Empire!

But then, once again, the severity of the message is softened, this time by the touching inclusion of the baby Jesus, securely held by God (the little person in the crook of his arm), and indeed God is pointing to the Virgin Mary, to offer his compassion and assurance that her son shall arise from death. Lastly, there is the cross at the very end of God's flag. This is a particular type of cross, called a 'cross pattée'.

It was used by the Roman church to signify divine authority; for example, it was the custom to put it in front of the signature of a bishop, when he issued an "Imprimatur". An Imprimatur is a formal declaration by the church that authorises a book as true and authorized presentation of the Catholic faith. So, Charlemagne's standard or Oriflamme, comes from God, and also has an additional attachment to it, signifying that it is authorized by God's representative.

The lower carving: key to the Externsteine's Celtic origin
Now we need to really carefully explore the remarkable carving that is to be seen just below this Christian scene. In illustration 9

you can see the relative size and positions of the carvings. The question arises, just what is the relationship of the carving in the lower register (or section) of the wall, to the Christian relief in the upper register? Although the overall wall relief is so unusual and spectacular, being the largest Christian relief from medieval times ever made, and arising from such potent political events, it is rarely critiqued in art books on European or Carolingian art.

This is a similar situation to that concerning the Great Pyramid, whose more striking features are seldom assessed by mainstream experts, but often too sensationally misinterpreted by amateur enthusiasts. Art historians generally make some brief comments on the Deposition from the Cross, and then they simply conclude that this lower scene belongs to the upper one, i.e., that it was carved at the same time. The lower carving is very hard to see, compared with the 9th century Christian scene above it, because it is badly deteriorated. This poor state of preservation is said to be due to the carving simply not having been completed. But is this correct? Is it an incomplete Christian carving, or is it an ancient Celtic work of art, a work of art that holds the key to the spiritual meaning of the Externsteine?

Well, first we need to note the relationship of this carving to the overall relief, by giving it a careful scrutiny, see illustration 10. When you visit the site, check it out for yourself. Is it hard to see because it has not been completed? An incomplete sculpture usually has its shapes only lightly cut into the rock, so these are not chiselled right down into the background layer. Or, if the depth of each feature has been chiselled out on an incomplete carving, then the fine details will not be present. The fine details are not on an incomplete carving, because these are not cut in until the final stage of the work is done.

A close look at this lower carving shows that it is in fact, complete. It has been completely carved, for the various parts of this scene have in fact been cut right into the background rock, just   as   deeply   as   the   scene   which   is   above   it.

93

10 **The lower register** of the carved wall; the dragon scene, very deteriorated through millennia of weathering.

But also the final stage of the carving is evident for its fine features have been carefully carved into these shapes. This can be seen for example, in the folds in the shawl around the woman's head, in the edge of the man's head cap, and in the edging of the dragon's lower beard. Another difference between the upper and the much older lower carving is that the general rock surface between the figures in the lower scene has not been carefully ground down to a smooth surface, unlike the similar areas in the well-defined setting for the Christian scene above. So the areas between the figures in the lower scene retain a similar unevenness to the areas above and to the right of the Christian scene, and elsewhere on this rock tower.

So the carving is very, very old, and has been damaged due to its extreme age, i.e., the millennia during which it has been exposed to the weather, and in addition, there appears to be damage caused by human hands, for example by Charlemagne's troops. So we can start to conclude that it is of Celtic origin, and that this scene is not just of Teutonic origin, and certainly it is not of Christian origin!

It goes back to the earlier, Celtic-Germanic peoples of pre-Christian Europe. On one of my visits, someone had painted the word 'Siegfried!' near this lower carving, out of frustration at it being defined as Christian. But both this Germanic enthusiast and the more conservative mainstream art historians are incorrect, it is neither Christian nor Teutonic. A further examination of the actual theme presented in this carving will give further clues as to its age. So, what was depicted here? Look at illustration 11.

11 The dragon Carving

Top

This outline, carefully worked out by Schröder, shows the features in the dragon scene of what can still be seen, so it has only minimal reconstruction. It has been coloured-coded by the author for further clarity. You can see its original features, and the two places (pale areas) where sections of the original stone carving have been obliterated over time.

Below

A sketch by the author, coloured-coded for clarity, which attempts to more fully reconstruct what was originally there.

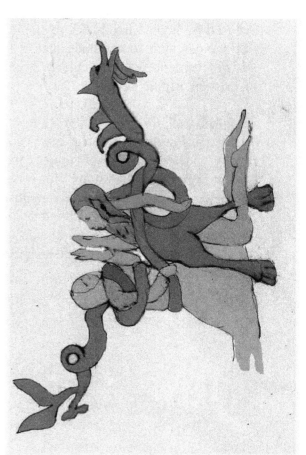

Reconstructing the damaged lower relief

These will give you the clearest possible view of what this fascinating scene once portrayed. The first illustration is an accurate outline, drawn over a photograph, and colour coded, showing what the scene once depicted, with the least possible addition of theoretical reconstruction. The coloured drawings in illustration 11 show two ways of going on to reconstruct the original scene. What do we see there? We see two people ensnared by a dragon. The man on the right seems to be naked, or perhaps has a short tunic around the middle, the lady is clothed, even having a fine shawl, and the monster is a dragon that has two legs, and a bearded head. The mainstream interpretation is that it is of the same age as the church carving above, and that it represents Adam and Eve and the Serpent who entered Paradise. However a closer consideration reveals that this is a simplistic, false conclusion.

It simply cannot be depicting the serpent in Paradise, tempting Eve. There are several reasons. Firstly, both Adam and Eve were naked in Paradise; they became clothed only after being expelled from the Garden of Eden. Secondly, in the Bible the serpent came into Paradise in order to tempt Adam and Eve in his most persuasive way, he did not overtly attack them, nor did he ever seize them. Nor is any such attack mentioned, in great contrast to the Germanic myths where dangerous dragons figure largely. Finally, it was a serpent, not a dragon that entered the Garden of Eden.

So, that leaves only one other vague basis to the incorrect attitude that it is a Christian artwork. If it were a Christian work of art, then Christian monks have depicted here a Saxon woman and man being ensnared by an evil monster. And, the scene above them speaks of how to get salvation from this predicament, i.e., through Christ. However, this line of reasoning has two problems. Firstly, the dragon, and the kneeling position and style of the two people are all carved very much in the Celtic style, and not in the Christian Carolingian style. Some good examples of Celtic artwork from early medieval times, or earlier can be seen in the Jelling stone, in Denmark.[18] It is obvious that this old Celtic style is present in the lower scene. And, since it is utterly unknown for artists in earlier ages, of one art genre, to carve in the style of another genre, one can conclude yet again that this lower scene is certainly not Christian.

Furthermore, the second problem is that, as we have noted, since this lower scene is so much more weathered, it is much older than the upper Christian scene, which dates from some time in Charlemagne's rule, perhaps about 805-810 AD. Since there was never any earlier period in time when a Christian carving would have been allowed at the Externsteine (!), the greatest of 'pagan' Celtic-Germanic sacred sites, we can again conclude that the carving is non-Christian.

It has also been rumoured that the upper carving was cut into the rock, to obliterate an earlier, Celtic one. Now, it is true that the Christian scene above has been carved in a prominent position, as a way to proclaim the predominance of the new religion over the Celtic religion of the Saxons. But it is unlikely that there was some other earlier Celtic carving there, as the Christian carving projects out to the same level as the older Celtic one. If an underlying scene had been erased with a chisel, then the new one would have to be carved much deeper back into the rock wall, than it actually is. So the Christian carving was cut onto a bare rock wall, with nothing else above it. So, this leaves us with the task of assessing the origins of this carving from an analysis of its theme.

Some people have concluded that it is a scene showing Siegfried or Sigurd, battling against a dragon, in order to rescue a fair maiden. This is a theme that forms a significant part of the Nordic-Celtic sagas. It is found in different versions throughout the old German and Icelandic texts, such as the Nibelungenlied (The song of the Nibelungs), and the Lay of Fafnir, Gripnir's Prophecies, etc. However, this it cannot be. It is not a depiction of a Teutonic myth, it is not the battle of Siegfried against the

---

[18] A good photo is at http://www2.vobs.atg/ball-online/ABOUT/103-0336

dragon. This is quite obvious once we reconstruct the scene, and then can see just what was originally carved there. A careful look at the features of this scene reveals that the man's right arm, his sword arm, actually has no sword! It is raised up, empty; and also it is held up, like the left arm of the woman, in despair and anguish. So this scene is depicting two people, a man and a woman, being ensnared by a dragon, a symbol of evil forces.

Now, we have considered that if the scene were Christian, it would be saying that these pagans are entrapped in an untrue religion or at least, in a morally unenlightened state. But, we have shown that this is incorrect, as the carving is a Celtic work of art. And besides, such a hostile slur on the religion of the conquered Saxon's would surely be ill advised for an Emperor trying to consolidate his rule. Moreover, it would contradict the inclusive message of the above scene, wherein two Saxon men are helping at the grim events of Golgotha. But, anyway, the idea of a Christian origin can be dismissed. It is a much older piece of art.

Nidhoggr; a warning of the ethical challenge

So, this scene depicts an ancient Celtic carving. But what is it depicting? This feature is about the teaching in mystical circles, that people who want a high esoteric spirituality, need to become aware that an ethical transformation is demanded of them. The lower qualities actually become more obvious and intrusive, as one's attitudes to ethics, and one's conscience, become more refined and alert. This includes the fact that the contrast between one's earthly attitudes and the higher spiritual realities become more apparent. This fact, of a hidden layer of self-seeking tendencies, even of potentially deeply unethical impulses lurking in the human soul, has to be acknowledged and encountered. A verse from the Edda speaks of this:

> More serpents lie under the roots of the Ash-tree,
> Than the foolish can imagine….
> The ash-tree Yggdrasil
> Endures more injury than people realize

A deer eats its upper leaves,
underneath Nidhoggr gnaws at it;
and it decays at the sides.   (Sayings of Grimnir)
(trans. the author)

In the Edda, Niddhoggr is a dark, menacing dragon, who is associated with the dark elves and dwells in murky Nifelheimr. Since the Celtic priesthood considered the human being to be an offshoot of the larger nine-fold cosmos, with its many beings, then it is quite possible that to them, Niddhoggr and other sinister things are, to some extent, active in the lower tendencies of the human being. Just as this dragon gnaws away at the roots of the cosmos, the great Tree of Life, so too, in the less conscious part of our soul its lower instincts, similar unwholesome influences are at work.

On approaching the site about 3,500 years ago, **one would note the stark scene of two people ensnared by a large dragon**. A solitary scene, but all the more impressive for being alone on the otherwise huge bare rock wall. It appears to represent the given human condition, as seen from the stern and lofty perspective of the priesthood. This depicts the challenging attitude of the senior priests towards that person, whether man and woman, who has not yet become spiritually renewed through the processes that they offer.[19]

The implication of the scene showing Niddhoggr ensnaring people appears to be that the religious rites of the Celtic priesthood can release the human being from an oppressive influence. So, we conclude that the solution to the lower carving is that it was a Celtic scene, pre-dating the Teutonic tribes. It is an admonition about Niddhoggr, the un-spiritual lower qualities, and how one's soul, with its potential higher qualities, are unfree whilst ensnared in it, and how the task of the person seeking spirituality involves conquering this.

---

[19] This same perspective is found in Biblical texts, and is referred to as 'the fallen state' of humanity.

In fact, it is possible that the carving is referred to in the verse we quoted above, "…an eagle hovers above the hall of Odhin". The rest of the verse, has more to say about Nidhoggr in connection with the appearance of the sanctuary of Odhin,

> Easy it is for those who come to Odhin
> to recognize his hall –
> an outcast* is placed   (*lit. a wolf)
> to the west of the door,
> and an eagle hovers above.   (trans. the author)

The figure of Nidhoggr is to the west of the entrance to the chamber, and the eagle carving. Often in sacred texts, the composer uses a kind of veiled way of saying something, a second meaning is interwoven in the words. Something very intriguing occurs here in this verse for the Edda. The priests who composed these verses used a word here for 'wolf' which is different to the ordinary term in old Icelandic for wolf (ulfr), such as when the verses speak about the wolf Skioll. It is the word, *vargr*, which derives from the term for warning or for an admonition, *vara*. (29)

So when people read or heard the verse recited, the word *vargr* called up the associated meaning of 'beware' or ostracized. In fact it often meant 'wolf' only in a symbolic way, because it was used of an ostracized or despised or criminal person. There was a phrase amongst the old Teutonic people that embodied this. Someone who was outcast was called "ein Wolf im Heiligtum" – "a wolf in the sanctuary". This idiomatic phrase is a bit abbreviated, and actually means, someone who was not allowed or not welcome in the sanctuary. (17) A similar but more detailed scene warning of this same spiritual condition is depicted on the walls of a mystical site far away in the Lasta highlands of Ethiopia. This is a sacred site unique in the Christian world, from the 13th century.[20] This required struggle against Niddhoggr, so

---

[20]The only English language book ever written about the hidden meaning of this place is my companion volume in this series: Great Sacred Sites Series: **Lalibela in 13th century Ethiopia.**

100

dramatically depicted here at the Externsteine is another indication of the spiritual nature of this sacred site. So, we can conclude that some of this artwork dates from perhaps 1,500 before Christ, and other features from the La Tené Celtic A-B period (450-300 BC).

An overview of the original features
This conclusion is supported further from a remarkable feature in the upper chamber, only part of which we looked at earlier. Now the verse also says that there is an eagle at Odhin's sanctuary. Above an opening in the rock wall was, and indeed still is today, a large carving of the outline of an eagle. The eagle itself has been cut out, presumably on orders from Charlemagne, but the soldiers overlooked the fact that if you cut out an eagle, you leave behind an eagle shape (!). So I have drawn the shape in again, see illustration 12. The eagle indicates that here was the sacred temple of Odhin, which was probably designed to be an earthly reflection of the great spiritual hall of Asgard. Asgard is the name for the realm of the Nordic gods.

And moreover, in some of his spiritual encounters with hostile beings Odhin transformed himself into an eagle. The eagle indicates that here was the sacred temple of Odhin, which was probably designed to be an earthly reflection of the great spiritual hall of Asgard. Asgard is the realm of the Nordic gods. The acolyte would have well known, as The Sayings of Grimnir declare, "…an eagle hovers above the hall of Odhin."

The Edda tells us that on the top of the great Tree of the Cosmos hovers an eagle, and it is even said that on its forehead there sits a hawk. This symbolizes the all-seeing, all-knowing power of Odhin. Subsequently, in some of his spiritual encounters with hostile beings, Odhin transformed himself into an eagle.

So let's now get an overview of what was once present here at the Externsteine, see illustrations 12a,b,c where the ancient site has been reconstructed, to show how approximately how it

101

looked long ago. Huge sandstone columns, with mysterious faces and profiles of various beings; amongst these are the sacred deer of the sun, from whom the essence of our earthly life-energies derives. And there is also Odhin's human vessel, attuned to the cosmic tree, seeking to obtain the enlightenment needed to bring spiritual wisdom to his people.

Grottos have been carved out of the columns, for spiritual rituals, and there is an upper chamber that provided exact observation of cosmic energies operative during the seasons by identifying the summer solstice; and there was also a remarkable astronomical observatory, identifying the lunar nodal cycle. Standing up, tall and impressive in front of Column Two, is the huge Irmin Column, symbol of the great Creator and his many-layered Tree of Life.

To the right of this solemn symbol was a portal to a smaller cupola grotto, and this was guarded by the one eyed Odhin. There is also an opening into the main grotto, which is 11 yards long by 3.3 yards wide (10m x 3m). It was here no doubt that spiritual rituals took place, and advice made available from the seeress, the revered Weleda, on questions of the spirit, and on crucial national issues. Above this chamber is the eagle carving, and to the west of this is the dragon Niddhoggr with his two victims. Finally, on the far eastern side is the fascinating spiritual sarcophagus, where the three-day journey of the acolyte into the Otherworld was carried out. So the acolyte is aware, on approaching this site, that it is sacred to Odhin and that here is a place where one may have an experience of spiritual realities.

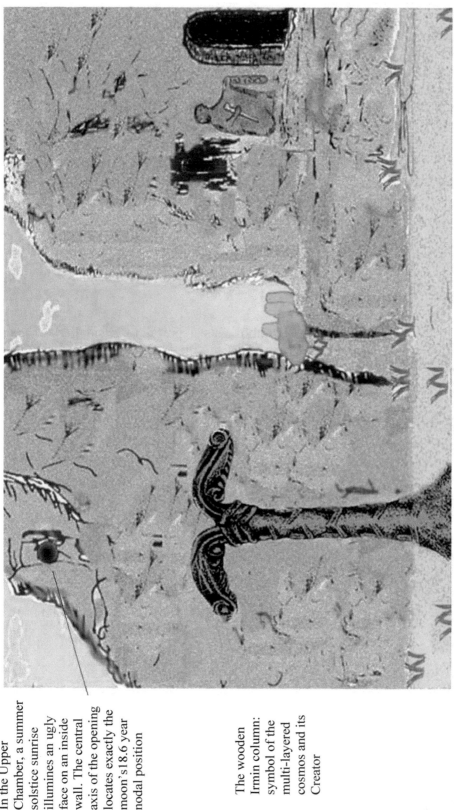

In the Upper Chamber, a summer solstice sunrise illumines an ugly face on an inside wall. The central axis of the opening locates exactly the moon's 18.6 year nodal position

The wooden Irmin column: symbol of the multi-layered cosmos and its Creator

12a The Externsteine's central features about 1,500 BC. The Irmin column & Odhin guards the chamber.

Odhin's eagle indicates the main chamber.

Westward of the entrance is Nidhoggr, holding captive 2 people.

12B On the bare rock wall a dragon (the lower self) ensnares a man and a woman. The acolyte prepares for a cathartic struggle.

12C The full scene: it probably looked like this. The sarcophagus is not visible in this view.

Chapter Seven: The meaning of the solar & lunar alignments

The distorted face in the upper chamber

We saw earlier how this chamber provided a way to know when the midsummer solstice occurred as well as the lunar nodes. However there is still more to this chamber than the remarkably accurate alignments of its aperture. Most of the rear of the chamber was been destroyed in the 8th century, but on the rear wall, towards the north, are two very intriguing features. Low down on one wall, near to the ground, is a carving of a strange ugly face, see illustration 13. And higher up is a small depression cut into the wall, which shows no details of any kind.

The face itself was certainly carved sometime in antiquity; it is much older than the Renaissance, and although it has some resemblance to baroque art, this is misleading. For it also has some resemblance to artworks of 2,500 years ago, such as those from the Hellenistic era. A good example of which is the face reflected in the wine goblet from the Dionysian villa of the Mysteries at Pompeii, see illustration 13. This unusual art theme appears to convey a mystical view of the lower qualities in human consciousness. This face is involved in what happens when the sun's rays enter the chamber on the summer solstice.

Let's see what happened in this chamber on June 21st. Karl Hublow reports that on the morning of the summer solstice (you would be in deep darkness if its roof and wall were still there). As the sun rises, you would see some light enter the round hole, and shine as a small oval glow on the rear wall (which is still there). Then, while you look at this glow, as the sun slowly rises up and moves in an easterly direction, this oval of light moves in a westerly direction along the rear wall. It becomes more and more shaped like an arrow, over a period of five hours. And then, just before it disappeared, it lights up the ugly face, down there on the north-westerly wall. Then you would again be in darkness. (30) A remarkable experience which was deliberately prearranged by the Celtic priests!

13 A

The ugly head from the Villa of the Mysteries, at
Pompeii, ca. 100 AD.
Not identical to the Externsteine face, but yet
similar in quality.
Like the one in the initiatory chamber at the Externsteine, this Italian image from the Dionysian
Mysteries, represents the Lower Self,
manifesting in connection with alcohol (a key
theme in the Dionysian cult.)

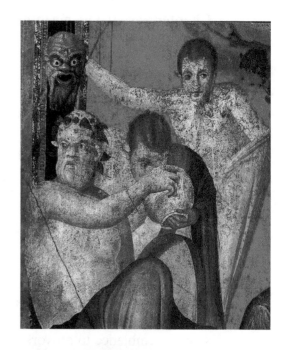

13B Somewhat damaged, but still clearly discernible is this ugly face. Representing the Lower
Self, this image is lit up at the Midsummer sunrise, as the sunlight enters the chamber.

It means that the person would have seen, just before the darkness descends again, for a few seconds, this striking image of an ugly face. Is it a symbol of his or her own shadow side or lower self; the part of the mind which is held by Niddhoggr? So, it seems that the ancient Celtic priests at the Externsteine were concerned with what lies 'within' in the human being, not just what lies 'without' in the cosmos. This chamber is a spiritual chamber, which provided valuable insights into not only the lunar nodes and other cosmic activity, but also into the deeper recesses of the soul.

The dragon which so graphically ensnares humanity, in the scene carved on the bare rock wall outside, has now been glimpsed in this private moment in a somewhat human form, and, as the chamber again becomes plunged into darkness, one is left in the dark chamber contemplating how to deal with one's own shadow self.

Careful analysis of the sun's motion on the summer solstice shows that this feature was created about 4,000 years ago; that is, it goes back to 2,000 BC. This is known because astronomical calculations of the angle of sun's rays on the summer solstice reveal that it would be striking the wall too high up to light this face, prior to 2,000 BC; but any time thereafter for many centuries it would strike it accurately. (23)

The existence of this strange feature is probably due to the conviction of earlier peoples that the seasonal cycle was not just a physical process caused by the motions of the Sun and the Earth. They felt that there were also changes in the subtle energies as the seasons changed. And, perhaps it was these changes on the subtle levels that produce the special ambience that each season has. Moreover to the ancient Celts, spiritual beings both malignant and good emerged to affect people, or receded away, according to the seasons. For example, the winter solstice was a sacred time, especially the nights. In continental Europe and in the British Isles, it was said that some type of sacred spiritual light was present, in the darkness of winter;

whereas the summer time was the opposite, in the bright dreamy warmth, was some kind of sinister force.

It is worth noting here that this chamber, like the one down at ground level that has the cupola shaped ceiling, was also in fact a shadow-chamber, in that it shielded the person inside from the sunlight. This could mean that the priestesses and priests inside this chamber were to enact rites at the midsummer solstice, shaded from the blinding summer light.

This shaded situation, inside the chamber, resembles similar chambers in Carnac and Britain. Inside these chambers the priests may have tried to perceive subtle spiritual qualities, which are otherwise invisible in the bright sunlight. A strange idea, but one which conceals a really significant key to understanding the Megalithic sites especially the amazing design of Stonehenge, which has puzzled researchers for centuries.[21]

Seasonal awareness & the upper chamber
The architectural accuracy in the design of this chamber enabled the priests to monitor various astronomical motions, as we have seen. But the alignment of this chamber is even more sophisticated than this. For astoundingly, the time of the day on the summer solstice when the light illuminates this ugly face, is exactly the same time when the sun rises on the spring equinox and on the autumn equinox. Furthermore, in the process of the light shining in on the summer solstice sunrise and moving along the wall, and illumining the ugly face, it also lights up a small depression cut into the northerly wall – and it does this at the very time of the day when the sun rises on the winter solstice!

So, on that summer solstice day, seated inside the chamber, you have a brief reminder of the other three key points in the year, the winter solstices, and the two equinoxes. (30) These

---

[21] The companion volume to this book, Great Sacred Sites Series 3, Stonehenge: a Handbook to the world's greatest Megalithic site, explains what these darkened chambers are designed for, using special graphics showing the sarsen stones at Stonehenge.

alignments to the complex movements of the sun and moon that influence the seasons are also prominent in Megalithic sacred sites. The Megalithic people are those people who built Stonehenge and many stone chambers across Carnac and Britain. They share a similar nature spirituality to that of the Continental Celts.

The wobble stone on Column Four
We noted earlier that there is a stone weighing several tons perched precariously on top of the stone outcrop known as Column Four, which has the carving of Odhin on one side, and of the sacred deer Eikthyrnir on the other side. When you see it at the site, it is very striking, and one notes with relief that State authorities have arranged for half-hidden steel rods to hold it securely in place. In fact already early in the 19th century it was cemented onto the rock below. This feature is another indicator that the Externsteine was a site sacred to the Celts, as these wobble stones are found in sites that were sacred to the Celtic and the Megalithic peoples.

Pre-historians have noted these stones in such sites, and the very striking fact that some of them can actually be moved by the touch of one hand, even though they may weigh many tons. For example, the antiquarian John Ackerman, in the 19th century, mentions the Agglestone wobble stone, on the island of Purbeck (UK), which has an estimated weight of 500 tons, and can be made to begin a rocking motion by the push of one hand! (31)

Ancient historians such as Pliny and Apollonius Rhodius have noted such stones, and written of how a gentle push, but not a violent shove, could set them rocking. (32) Scientists, intrigued as to how such huge rocks can basically be stable for millennia, and yet so easily moveable, have examined such stones, to try to ascertain their precise geometrical shaping underneath, at the point where they balance on the lower rock. (33)

It is a fact also that in antiquity such special rocks were often viewed by the priests as having a certain energetic quality, and this lead to them being revered, or integrated into a sacred site.

Fascinating folklore about sacred rocks from all over the world, show that people once believed that during a ritual, through the powers of the shaman or Druid, such rocks could be put into motion or even 'speak' (in wind-like tones). It was also believed sometimes that such rocks could come to life, in some eerie way, at key times of the moon's cycle or at a solstice. The chief oracle of the ancient Greeks, at Delphi, and of the Mandan Indians of America, and of many other peoples, had a large stone at the site of the oracle or temple (not necessarily a wobble stone, but in some way striking, such as, being a meteor). (34)

So, it is very likely that the Externsteine wobble stone was also regarded in this way, and played a role in the religious life of the people, being put into motion by the priests, at special times. Modern mystical groups believe that part of such a ritual could involve the rock being made to move by some subtle mental power of the high priest, and perhaps this is what the tribes people in earlier ages believed.

Here at the Externsteine, it is very likely that as part of sacred rituals, the will of Odhin was made manifest to the priests below, through the mysterious motions of this rock. This would have been a very impressive experience to the people assembled down below!

Conclusion: the age and significance of the Externsteine
The tall sandstone columns of the Externsteine were used and developed over a long period of time by different peoples in northern Europe. But millennia before, the inhabitants of this part of Europe used the Externsteine (and the nearby Falcon rock) as a site from which to experience the seasonal cycle. The Urnfield people or primal Celts, about 3,000-2,500 BC used this striking rock outcrop as their most sacred site. Over the centuries they gave it more sophisticated features, carving specific figures into the rocks to teach their religion over many centuries, they developed the site, creating such features as the figure of Odhin hanging from the tree of life.

They also carved the dragon scene warning of the lower nature, and formed the spiritual grottos, and eventually the upper observation chamber, and down on the ground, the spiritual sarcophagus. These may have been influenced by their priests' knowledge of similar features in other esoteric streams, such as those of Mediterranean sacred sites.

Then in the Hellenistic era, around 300 BC, as the Teutonic tribes, the ancestors of today's German people, became a recognizable ethnic group in northern Germany, the Externsteine with its Celtic religious origins became a unifying focal point for the life and needs of these Teutonic tribes. The site was regarded as too sacred to be used as a habitation, it was reserved for the religious rituals and solemn gatherings for the tribes people. The high priestess, the Weleda seeress, helped them in the ongoing battle against the troops of the Roman Empire. It was still the central sacred site for the Germanic tribes in Charlemagne's time, 1,000 years later and, in an attempt to destroy their will to resist, he damaged the many features of the site including its Irmin Column, in 772 AD.

It was probably from the Externsteine in particular that the spiritual insights were gained which underlie the Edda, one of the world's great mythological-religious texts. That is, at the Externsteine the spiritual insights of the priestesses or priests concerning the nature and significance of various spiritual

112

beings were experienced, and communicated in confidential teaching, or in graphic forms on the rocks, and in rites; and of course, they were also taught in the form of myths.

The precise astronomical observation sites created here allowed the priesthood to regulate the nature-based life of the peoples. From this the myths were created as a way to educate the tribes-people, and after some millennia of being orally recounted, as the spiritual capacity to have these experiences dwindled, the myths were given their literary resting place in the Edda. The Externsteine is one of the few really great sacred sites of ancient times that have survived. It is sufficiently intact, to allow us to still experience the wonderful, enchanted world of the old Celtic peoples.

Appendix

The original Latin report in the Annales Laurissenses Maiores, part of the Frankish Imperial Annals.

[772] DCCLXXII. Tunc domnus Carolus mitissimus rex sinodum tenuit ad Warmatiam. Et inde perrexit partibus Saxoniae prima vice, Eresburgum castrum coepit, ad Ermensul usque (as far as) pervenit (arrive at) et ipsum (itself) fanum (sanctuary) destruxit et aurum vel argentum, quod ibi repperit (he discovered), abstulit (he removed) . Et fuit siccitas magna, ita ut aqua deficeret in supradicto loco, ubi Ermensul stabat; et dum voluit ibi duos aut tres praedictus gloriosus rex stare dies fanum ipsum ad perdestruendum et aquam non haberent, tunc subito divina largiente gratia media die cuncto exercitu quiescente in quodam torrente omnibus hominibus ignorantibus aquae effusae sunt largissimae, ita ut cunctus exercitus sufficienter haberet.

More About: the little child on the carving
 Since the Christian carving was made after the conversion of the fierce Saxon leader Wittekind to Christianity, it is just possible that the little child that God is holding represents something else, and not the baby Jesus, as a way to convey compassion to the Virgin Mary in her grief. For an early medieval writer, Radbert, of the very influential Benedictine abbey of Corvey, near to the Teutoburger Forest, has described in several treatises for the monks of an abbey, a mystical idea about the mass. That during the Mass, as the bread and the wine become transformed (the famous Transubstantiation concept), they become perceptible as a small child to people in the church. Now, as Gesänger points out, it is reported in legendary material that the famous Saxon chieftain, Wittekind, prior to being converted peered discreetly inside a tent where the Mass was being celebrated, and saw this mystical child figure.

However, this concept is not uncommon in mystical Christian writings of the Middle Ages, so it is only a small possibility that the little child in God's arm might refer to this. Indeed such a legend has the hallmarks of convenient political-religious myth, for which the Church became well known. It is possible that it does refer to this mystical child, but we conclude that it is much more likely for it to refer to the baby Jesus. In any event, on this point of the role of the abbey of Corvey, it may well be the case that the monks who carved the Christian relief at the Externsteine were from this abbey, as Mathes suggests. (16)

The dragon slaying by Siegfried near the Teutoburger Forest
Although we know that the scene in the lower register does not depict a dragon slayer, the story of a hero slaying a dragon did provide inspiration to the struggling acolyte. This myth presents an initiated person successfully conquering their own lower self. The battle of St. George against the dragon became such a primary theme in English literature. And in German literature, the adventures and slaying of the dragon, by Siegfried or Sigurd, a dragon who was threatening a fair maiden, was a core theme for many centuries in the Germanic world. This story is not just about courage and the virtue of being a valiant knight; it also has a deeper, spiritual meaning. On this level, it is about the effort of the 'self', considered as masculine, to rescue a princess, (i.e., the soul,) who is considered as feminine. The hero is either Sigurd or Siegfried, and the name of the heroine may be Kriemhilde or Gudrun or Sigrdrifa or Brynhild (the latter is called Brünnhilde in Wagner's opera, the Ring of the Nibelungen).

A further point here is that the legend of the slaying of the dragon Fafnir by Sigurd was given enhanced power in the imaginations of the Teutons, by specifying a location where the battle took place. The same was done for the Christians, with the legend of St. George slaying the dragon; the legend says that it was at Joppa in Palestine that St. George slew the dragon.

Likewise in the German world, it was a widely held belief, derived from the wonderful old saga, the Nibelungenlied, that Sigurd slew the dragon in an actual physical battle, in a place called the 'Gnita heath-land' (Gnitaheide). This was known in the 12th century, and was mentioned by an Abbott Nicolaus, who notes in his travel memoirs, written in 1150, as he left the Teutoburger Forest, "…this is the Gnita heath-land, where Sigurd slew Fafnir." So, to the Saxons this pivotal event in their myths, inspiring for the acolyte when understood on the mystical level, took place near the Teutoburger Forest, and hence not far from the Externsteine.

REFERENCES

1 Johannes Mundhenk, Forschungen zur Geschichte der Externsteine Bd.II, Verlag F. L.Wagner, Lemgo, 1980.

2 Ernst Wahle, Deutsche Vorzeit, Wissenschaftliche Buchgemeinschaft, Tübingen,1952

3 Ref: R Jähne, R. Linde, C. Woda, Licht in das Dunkel der Vergangenheit, Verlag für Regionalgeschichte, 2007

4 Cassius Dio, Roman History, bk. 55 & 56; available at: http://Penelope.uchicago.edu/Thayer/E/Roman/Texts/Cassius_D io

5 Tacitus, The Complete works of Tacitus, Modern Library, New York, 1942

6 Annales Regni Francorum (Annales Laurissenses Maiores) available at http://www.thelatinlibrary.com/annalesregnifrancorum.html

7 Einhard:Vita Karoli Magni, edit. Ludwig Gompf, Vlg Aschendorf, Münster,1971, and P. Schaff, History of the Christian Church, Vol. IV AD 509-1073, Eerdmans, Grand Rapids, 1910.

8 In Fritz Vater, Eine Studie zum Feldzug des Jahres 772, Vlg Hohe Warte. Franz v. Bebenberg, Pähl/Obb, 1954

9 The original Icelandic is in: *Die Lieder der Älteren Edda (Saemundar Edda)* hrsg., Karl Hildebrand, Ferdinand Schöningh Vlg, Paderborn, 1912. Fine translations and study texts include, *The Poetic Edda* by Carolyne Larrington, OUP, London, 1999; and *Die Edda Übertragen von Felix Genzmer*, Bd 2, Eugen Dierichs Vlg, Düsseldorf-Köln, *Altnordisches Elementarbuch*, Dr. F. Ranke, Walter de Gruyter & Co, Berlin 1949; *Die Edda Übertragen von Karl Simrock*, Deutsche Buch-Gemeinschaft, Berlin, 1926, *VollständigesWörterbuch zu den Liedern der Edda* von H.Gering, Halle, Vlg. der Buchhandlung des Waisenhauses, 1903.

10 Gylfis Verblendung, in Die Ältere Edda, übers. K Simrock; The Deluding of Glyfi, trans. M. Mallet, Northern Antiquities, trans. Bishop Percy, Henry G. Bohn, London, 1847

11 Snorri Sturluson The Prose Edda, trans., J. Young, Univ. Calif. Press, Berkeley,

1966; The Deluding of Glyfi, trans. M. Mallet, Northern Antiquities

12 Karl Simrock, Handbuch der Deutschen Mytholgie mit Einschluß der nordischen, Adolf Marcus, Bonn, 1874

13 Wessobrunner Prayer; A German Anthology, edit. C. Thomas, London,D. C. Heath & Co. 1910

14 Nancy Arrowsmith, A Field Guide to the Little People, Pan, 1978, p.136

15 J. Grimm, Deutsche Mythologie, Ullstein Materialien, Frankfurt-Main, 1981, and W. Mannhardt, Der Baumkultus der Germanen und ihrer Nachbarstämme,
Gebrüder Borntraeger, Berlin 1875

16 W. Mathes, Corvey und die Externsteine, Urachhaus, Stuttgart, 1982 & also
www.sternfreunde-muenster.de/pdf/andromeda001

17 K. Simrock, Handbuch der Deutschen Mythologie

18 Shamanism, A Reader, edit. Graham Harvey,_Routledge, 2002

19 Leonid Lar, The Process of Education of the Nenets Shamans; see the website, www.taraka.pl/index.php

20 Taliesin: shamanism and Bardic mysteries in Britain and Ireland, The Aquarian Press, London, 1991

21 Quoted by E. Davies, The mythology and rites of the British Druids, J. Booth, London, 1809, p. 409

22 J. E.A. Kroesen, The Sepulchrum Domini through the Ages; its form and function; Peeters, 2001, p 29

23 R. Speckner and C. Stamm, Das Geheimnis der Externsteine, Urachhaus, Stuttgart 2002.

24 Tacitus, The Complete Works, edit. M. Hadas, Random House N.Y. 1942, and Die Germanen, Ein Lexikon zur europäischen Frühgeschichte edit. H. Döbler, Bertelsmann Vlg, Berlin, 1975.

25 Benjamin Thorpe "The Yuletide Stories of the North; fireside tales of Sweden, Norway, Denmark and north Germany".

26 F.R. Schröder, Quellenbuch zur germanischen Religionsgeschichte, Berlin /Leipzig, 1933, p. 103; also on Wikipedia

27 See de.Wikipedia/irminsul

28 Hans Gesänger, Die Externsteine, Novalis Verlag, Schaffhausen, 1978

29 Die Lieder der Edda, Wörterbuch Bd. 2 edits. Simons & Gering ps. 1078 & 1080, Halle, 1903

30 Karl Hublow, Die Externsteine – Zwölf Fotopostkarten, Christengemeinschaft Vlg, Konstanz, 1968.

31 John. Y. Ackerman, Remains of antiquity of the Celtic, Romano-British and Anglo- Saxon periods, J. R. Smith, London, 1857

32 Pliny in Hist. Nat. Mb. ii.c. 96 & Apollonius Rhodes, Argonaut, lib.i. 1071(quoted by Ackerman)

33 Dammerman, W., *Celtische Wackelsteine*, in Physik in unserer Zeit, vol. 12, version 6, pp.178-180, Wiley-VCH Verlag, Wienheim, 1981, and R. Lindberg, *On the dynamic behavior of the wobble-stone*, in Acta Mechanica, Springer Verlag,Vienna, 1983.

34 P. Gardner, *Stones (Greek & Roman)*, Hastings Encyclopedia of Religion and Ethics, vol. 11, T & T Clark, Edinburgh, 1920 & C. Walker, Sites of Mystery & Imagination, Hamlyn, London, 1990.

SOME WORKS CONSULTED

Die Lieder der Älteren Edda (Icelandische urtext) Saemundar Edda Hrsg. Hildebrand, Redak. H. Gering, Vlg von Ferdinand Schöningh, Paderborn 1912 The Poetic Edda: Trans. by Carolyne Larrington, OUP, 1996 Die Edda: Felix Genzmer, Übers., E. Diererichs Verlag, 1979 Die Edda: Karl Simrock, Übers., Deutsche Buch-Gemeinschaft Gmb. Berlin, 1926 The Poetic Edda: essay on Old Norse Mythology, ed., P. L. Acker, C Larrington, Routledge, 2002.

H. R. E. Davidson, Gods & Myths of Northern Europe, Penguin, 1964.

H. Döbler, Die Germanen, Bertesmann Lexikon-Vlg, Berlin, 1975

E. Kitzinger, Early Medieval Art, British Museum, London 1983

C. Los, Die Altirische Kirche, Verlag Urachhaus, Stuttgart, no date

P. Schaff, History of the Christian Church, Vol. 4, Eerdmans, Grand Rapids, 1910

M. Mallet, Northern Antiquities of the ancient Scandinavians, trans. Bishop Percy,

I.A. Blackwell, London, 1847 Meyer's Konversations-Lexikon zweite Auflage, Redak. H. Meyer, Hildburghausen, 1866 Chief Seattle: The Great Chief sends word: [Perry's altered version] Chief Seattle: How can one sell the air? [William Arrowsmith's corrected version];edit. E. Gifford & R M Cook, The Book Publishing Company, Summertown, Tennessee 1992 Chief Seattle: Wir sind ein Teil der Erde, [German, a well nuanced version]; Walter-Verlag AG Olten, 1984

C. Thomas, An Anthology of German Verse, D.C. Heath, London, 1910

H. Voß, Altgermanische Lese, Alexander Fischer Vlg, Tübingen, 1929.

INDEX

Illustration credits:

Map adapted from: www.freeworldmaps/europa

1 With kind permission of Siegfried Schröder, on http://www.externstein-aarstein.de/die-bilder.html. Used by the kind permission of the photographer. The use by this author of these images does not imply support of my thesis by the owner of this picture.

2 Map adapted from: www.freeworldmaps/europa

3 With kind permission of the estate of Karl Hublow (1901-1979)

4 commons.wikimedia Description; Externsteine Date: 17 April 2009

Source: Flickr.com Author: **fienne-sfjienne** The use by me of the image does not imply support of my thesis by the owner of this picture

5 Top: With kind permission of the estate of Karl Hublow

5 Bottom: from the website of **Klearchos Kapoutsis** in Santorini Cyclades Greece http://klearchosguidetothegalaxy.blogspot.com/2008/11/blog-post_21.html; and re license see http://creativecommons.org/licenses/by3.0/ The use by me of the image does not imply support of my thesis by the owner of this picture

6A with kind permission of Siegfried Schröder, on http://www.externstein-aarstein.de/die-bilder.html. Used by the kind permission of the photographer. The use by this author of his images does not imply support of my thesis by the owner of this picture.

6B Siegfried Schröder

7 With kind permission of the estate of Karl Hublow

8 http://de.wikipedia.org/wiki/Datei:2007-06-06-Externsteine-33.jpg Owner Of Photo: R. **Engelhardt** Description: The Externsteine near Horn-Bad Meinberg, Germany Source: My own photo Camera: This Photo has been taken with a AIPTEK DV 6800 S camera. Date 6: June 2007 The use by me of this image does not imply support of my thesis by the owner of this picture

9A With kind permission of the estate of Karl Hublow

9B Marianne Klement-Speckner http://commons.wikimedia.org Description: die aufgerichtete Irminsul DATE 1996 SOURCE Eigenes Werk AUTHOR **Marianne Klement-Speckner** The use by me of this image does not imply support of my thesis by the owner of this picture

10 With kind permission of the estate of Karl Hublow

11a Siegfried Schroeder

11b the author
12 the author
13A Commons Wikimedia
http://commons.wikimedia.org/wkik/File:Villa_dei_Misteri_VI_-
_1.jpg Description: Fresco from the Sala di Grande Dipinto Sc. 6
DATE 21 February 2009 SOURCE Marisa R. Panetta (ed) Pompeji.
Geschichte, Kunst und Leben in der versunkenen Stadt, Belser,
Stuttgart 2005 ISBN 3-7630-2266-X p. 319 AUTHOR **Wolfgang
Rieser**
13B With kind permission of the estate of Karl Hublow

Printed in the USA
CPSIA information can be obtained
at www.ICGtesting.com
LVHW071958131223
766150LV00048B/922